THE
STROUD VALLEYS
IN THE
GREAT WAR

THE FIVE VALLEYS GREAT WAR
RESEARCHERS GROUP

EDITED BY CAMILLA BOON

The
History
Press

First published 2017

The History Press
The Mill, Brimscombe Port
Stroud, Gloucestershire, GL5 2QG
www.thehistorypress.co.uk

British Library Cataloguing in Publication Data.
A catalogue record for this book is available from the British Library.

ISBN 978 0 7509 7054 9

Typesetting and origination by The History Press
Printed in Great Britain

CONTENTS

FOREWORD

National identity is alive and well. Local history societies flourish. Genealogists search for roots and ancestors. The commemoration of the First World War centenary provided a great incentive for historical research, as I found at an exhibition in Brimscombe in the summer of 2015, with local Great War servicemen and women detailed and pictured in Stroud district villages. That was only part of it. Names matter.

Edwin Budding was unknown in the Westminster village. He was an engineer building and repairing machines in local cloth mills. He was on to a world-beater. On 31 August 1830 he patented 'a new combination and application of machinery for the purpose of cropping or shearing the vegetable surface of lawns, grass-plats and pleasure grounds'. This was the world's first lawnmower. He got the idea for his lawnmower from the cross-cutting machines that were used to finish woollen cloth. Scythes were used before his invention. Think of that, members of the MCC (Marylebone Cricket Club) at Lords, or designers of garden cities, or when you next cut your grass at home.

A beer was named after him, produced by a local craft brewery, itself a reinstatement of identity. The old Stroud Brewery, a matter of local pride, was shut. It wasn't required by big business any more. But now on a Saturday night folk can buy Budding beer at a renewed Stroud Brewery in quart jugs and join their family, friends and dogs in a hubbub of jollity and talk.

Do you know the paintings of Pieter Bruegel the Elder, and particularly the one of the peasant wedding in 1568? There they are sitting on benches at bare trestle tables, a medieval invention, and there they were on my Saturday night in the local village also on benches at bare trestle tables, just the same really. I was drinking a pint of Budding beer.

Every so often a pizza in the making from properly crafted flour would be tossed in the air in the adjacent kitchen, cooked, scrumptious, over a wood fire. Never before or since have I had one like it, so light and tasty.

I gave a talk in a village up the road, Brimscombe, where I was born in the same house as my father, who saw as a child a procession up the hill celebrating the relief of Mafeking. I am so old – 84 now – that I am regarded as an artefact myself, remembering what is now diligently researched and asked about – shops in the village, where they were, what they sold and who ran them.

People want to know. It is as if they are re-cultivating a field which has lain fallow for too long. My father's secondary school logbook from Brimscombe Polytechnic in 1909 recalls what has since been forgotten – education for work, not as theory. It could actually be the basis of a manual for teaching today. He has drawn in it the first aeroplane and writes that he made a model of it. Pupils of my old local grammar school, Marling, and the nearby Girls' High School recently helped to create and build a real aeroplane. The first jet in Britain and America to fly, made by the then Gloster Aircraft company, was powered by Whittle's engine – on which my uncle worked. He began work as an apprentice in the village boat-building company where one of my grandfathers was foreman and the other worked with members of the family on river vessels exported across the world. The canal where they were launched is currently being revived.

Only now are we realising what has been lost. It seems to me that there is a great willingness to learn from the past, not least that people matter in this hi-tech world. There is a new surge of vigorous local enterprise, shops and pubs that care, with eager staff, women these days as well as men.

My strong impression is that the real Britain which matters has been asleep, but is now waking up. The Five Valleys are wonderfully active and true to themselves, as this book shows.

You could call it a re-assertion of identity, of what we have been and are.

Peter Evans, 2017

INTRODUCTION

As the centenary of the Great War approached, local history societies wondered how best to commemorate the subject of the effects of the conflict on their own towns and villages. For many groups, the obvious point of departure was the war memorial standing – for much of the year barely regarded – in the middle of their community. Such neat lists of names, each one, however, represents a personal tragedy. 'Lest Ye Forget' warns the monument in Chalford. The trouble was that the individual men had been largely forgotten. So the researches began, using online resources, old newspapers and other documents. Local historians sat in their own homes, in the local libraries, in the Gloucestershire archives, gradually uncovering the stories and the characters behind the names. The wider story of the ripple effect of war came into focus – the knitting and sewing parties, the lighting restrictions, the food shortages, the effects on local industry, the VAD hospitals, the increased opportunities for women, the Volunteer Training Corps, the constant background of uncertainty and worry.

Realising that there were many overlaps in our researches, several of the local history societies came together to form the Five Valleys Great War Researchers Group, which has provided a happy and supportive framework in which to develop our ideas and continue working.

In 2015 an exhibition entitled 'Stroud District and its part in the Great War' was held at Brimscombe, to coincide with a visit from Tina Blackman of New Zealand. She had completed research on the Cole family, and especially her great-grandfather and his three brothers from Bourne House in Brimscombe, who had served in the conflict; three had died and were commemorated in her publication, *The Three Uncles: The Cole Brothers in the Great War*.

Local publisher The History Press exhibited at the event, as did many of the villages and towns represented within the Five Valleys Great War Researchers. Peter Evans, a distinguished journalist and leader-writer for *The Times*, retired now, gave a fascinating talk, evoking his childhood in Brimscombe between the wars. Other short lectures and presentations took place and from this arose the idea of a publication to bring the research to a wider audience. Not all areas would be included – some were publishing their own accounts of a particular village, others were disseminating information via the Internet, and some were intending to continue working until 2018. However, it is hoped that the following will provide an overview of our area at this momentous time. The copyright for each essay remains with the individual authors and every effort has been made to trace and acknowledge the many illustrations that appear in the book.

Camilla Boon and Diana Wall
The Five Valleys Great War Researchers Group, 2017

SETTING THE SCENE

The coronation of King George V and Queen Mary took place on 22 June 1911 and was a cause of much rejoicing in Stroud and the surrounding areas. The cousin of many kings and queens throughout Europe and ruler of a worldwide empire, George was seen as the epitome of a modern head of state. The communities of the Five Valleys, and indeed many much nearer the heart of government, could not anticipate the shadows of war which would soon be gathering.

Stroud was the natural hub of the parishes lying along the five river valleys (Frome, Stroudwater, Painswick, Nailsworth and Slad) and the higher land lying between. The geology of the area gave it its character – the Greater Oolite (limestone) forming the plateaux with the Liassic clays exposed in the valleys. The limestone supported prosperous farming, both arable and livestock, and many of the men in the upland parishes were agricultural workers. Stone was still extensively quarried, especially around Rodborough and Minchinhampton. Over the previous century the woollen industry had become concentrated in large, highly mechanised factories in the river valleys, such as Dunkirk and Longfords mills, but new industries moved in to the smaller mills, including iron-founding, shoddy-working, silk-throwing, and the manufacture of pins, walking sticks and ready-made clothing. The 1911 census shows the importance of these in the economy of the area. In Nailsworth bacon-curing, brewing and engineering became prominent, attracting workers from agriculture.

Stroud had been much enlarged during the nineteenth century, mainly as a result of better road infrastructures and the coming of first the canal and then the railway. In 1914 the town was continuing to attract commercial and indus-trial development. Nailsworth also grew into a small town and from the late years of the century Rodborough was encroached on by the suburbs of Stroud, but much of the area remained predominately rural, with Minchinhampton, Painswick and Bisley becoming favoured residential areas.

It was from this background that men answered the call to arms at the outbreak of the Great War. Thanks to successive Education Acts the rural population was literate, advances in medicine and diet meant that few would be refused enlistment on health grounds, and the strong community spirit of the Five Valleys ensured that there was a network of support for the troops.

The following chapters from the Five Valleys Great War Researchers Group explore these themes in greater detail.

Diana Wall, 2017

1

UNINTENDED CONSEQUENCES

THE STROUD HOME FRONT, 1914-1918

MARION HEARFIELD

In August 1914 the local newspapers were full of enthusiastic support for Stroud's young men as they queued to volunteer for Lord Kitchener's Army. There were rallies and public meetings and promises, cheerful farewells and tearful farewells, and a real expectation that the war would not last long and the boys would all soon be home.

At that time, the *Stroud News* was published on a Friday, so there had been several days to digest the news when the first wartime issue was published on 7 August. That edition conveyed a vivid sense of a changed world, where the Territorials had suddenly been called up, shows and railway excursions cancelled, horses requisitioned, and there had been panic-buying (particularly of sugar and flour, strongly deprecated by the paper's editor).

When war was declared, all the banks closed for three days to prevent people withdrawing their money. When they reopened, new paper banknotes (£1 and 10*s*) had replaced gold sovereigns. The paper reported:

> Never, perhaps, has a great war been started in a more serious and sober spirit than this. Only the youthful who cannot appraise the terrible significance of war have so far exhibited the excitement which has characterised the mobilisation scenes in many of the great Continental towns.

STROUD JOURNAL" CARTOON.

JOHN BULL: "Good gracious, madam, are you intending to open a grocer's shop?"

WEALTHY PANIC PURCHASER: "No, I merely laid in sufficient stores to last during the war, before the prices went up.

JOHN BULL: "Yes, and by your selfish conduct you have made the situation much worse for your poorer neighbours. You are an enemy to your country, madam.

A cartoon decrying hoarding. (Courtesy of the Stroud News and Journal*)*

BELGIAN REFUGEES

Belgian refugees had fled the advancing Germans in 1914 and, within the space of six months, 250,000 Belgian refugees were found homes in the UK. They gave worried families something practical to do; if they could not look after their own sons then at least they could look after other displaced people. By early 1915 about 200 people were being looked after in and around Stroud.

The *Stroud News* of 11 September 1914 reported that fifty Belgian refugees arrived 'last Wednesday' at the invitation of Lady Howard of Castle Godwin, Painswick. They were met by Father Fitzgerald and given supper at the Convent (an accompanying black and white photograph of the event hides the fact that the hastily-hung Belgian flag was upside down!).

Local committees sprang up and provided clothes and food, lent furniture, identified lodgings or whole cottages for the bewildered and often angry visitors who had been forced to abandon their quiet lives and homes and been bundled into a different country with a different language. Jobs were found and compromises made on all sides, though it was not always easy. One family was housed at Selsley Vicarage. Gabrielle West, the 24-year-old vicar's daughter, wrote in her diary how difficult and demanding 'her' family was. But she jumped to their defence when the local committee wanted to move them to another house in two days' time without any consultation.

On New Year's Eve 1914, Lady Marling and a committee of seven ladies arranged an entertainment at Stroud's Subscription Rooms for '200 of our friends from Belgium staying in the district'. The hall was lavishly decorated by builder Philip Ford and helpers with gaily coloured flags and a 'gorgeous Christmas tree decorated with all manner of fancy articles and fairy candles'. There was a conjuror, a concert of songs accompanied by Mr S.W. Underwood, presents for every child, a 'bountiful supper' and, finally, the floor was cleared for dancing. In the adjacent column the newspaper listed the most recent dead and wounded soldiers from the Gloucestershire Regiment. Life was oddly fragmented.

SPY FEVER

A feature of the unsettled atmosphere during the first year of the war was the hostility and suspicion meted out to those who had foreign-sounding names. One incident concerned Mr and Mrs Jagger, who ran the Cosy Restaurant in Nelson Street. On 4 June 1915 they placed an 'Important Notice' in the *Stroud News* that stated that they were both of English birth and English parentage. They offered a reward of £5 for information leading to the conviction of the person or persons who had circulated the untrue and slanderous statement that they were Germans (the 1911 census shows that Mr Jagger had been born in Cumberland and his wife was a Yorkshirewoman). William Rothenstein, the distinguished artist then living in Far Oakridge, came in for similar treatment, to the extent that he (briefly) changed his name to Rutherston in 1916.

RECRUITMENT

The local newspaper editors had the unenviable and wearying task of encouraging enlistment, explaining shortages, defusing tensions and reporting on every trench death whilst exhorting their readers to carry on supporting the war effort because Britain *was* in the right and the evil enemy *would* be vanquished. They reported columns and columns of speeches, resolutions and committee meetings where much was discussed but often too little achieved. They published 'Letters to the Editor' – some of which make uncomfortable reading today. At a recruiting rally in August 1915, Lieutenant Fedden told the

National Registration card issued to shipbuilder's apprentice Stanley Evans, who had just started work at Abdela & Mitchell in Brimscombe. (Courtesy of Peter Evans)

women in his audience that if their sons were not already fighting in Flanders they should go down on their knees and beg them to go. When an indignant voice protested that she had five sons at the front already, she was congratulated briskly and told to make her friends do the same.

In July 1915 everyone between the ages of 15 and 65 not in military service had to complete a grey National Register form with their name, age, marital status, and a range of occupation codes – forty different groups for men, and thirty-six for women – ranging from unskilled agricultural labourers though clerks to bankers and professionals. 'No person may regard himself as too exalted or too humble to append his signature to the form, for all have equal obligations to the State' (*Stroud News*, 6 August 1915). The results were in by September 1915 and everyone was given a Registration Card.

The government introduced the Military Service Act on 27 January 1916. Voluntary enlistment was stopped and all British-resident men aged between 19 and 41 were deemed to have enlisted on 2 March 1916. Like it or not, they had been conscripted.

Conscripted men were not given a choice of regiment or unit, although if a man preferred the navy it got priority to take him. In May 1916 this Act was extended to married men, and the lower age dropped to 18.

TRIBUNALS

Compulsion brought disagreement, of course, and hundreds asked for deferment, if not complete exclusion. Stroud's Urban and Rural Military Tribunals, composed mainly of JPs and other pillars of the local community, aided by Lieutenant John Wood as military representative, held their first meetings at the end of February 1916. Claimants were anonymous to begin with, but from

30 June they were named. Here is a summary of a typical Stroud Urban District Tribunal session, held just after Christmas on 29 December 1916, by which time the format and tone of the proceedings was well-established:

· Messrs Bowstead and Co. wished to renew the exemption granted in Sept last to James Devlin (aged 40) married, manager of their Stroud branch at Hound Brand Works in Lansdown, wholly employed on Government work. He had been passed for garrison duty at home and conditional exemption was given.

· R. Townsend and Co. of Stratford Mills, oil and cake manufacturers, appealed on behalf of two of their labourers, both 24, both classified C2. A delay of one month was agreed. They also appealed on behalf of their married seed and corn buyer, E.J. Dash (aged 32). His exemption was granted until 31 March.

· Cotswold Stores Ltd argued that their slaughterman Arthur Neal, 37, married, classified C1, was in a reserved occupation. He was granted three months' exemption.

· Stroud Brewery, appealing for their married mineral water maker, J.T. Vernall (41), passed for garrison duty at home, was not successful, though call-up would be delayed for a month.

· Lieutenant Wood pressed strongly for W.G. Dyer (aged 41), a married carter working for Wood and Rowe coal merchants. His case was supported by Stroud Urban District Council because he was a member of the town fire brigade. Despite this special pleading, his exemption was refused as long as a substitute carter could be found.

· The case of Charles Osborne (aged 34) marine store dealer of Tower Hill, Stroud, was refused, as was that of Charles Watkins, a married tailor's machinist (aged 37), who appealed on personal grounds (what these were is not revealed, as the case was heard *in camera*).

· Eastmans butchers sought exemption for two of their men, F.C. Lawson (aged 40), manager of the sausage factory, and S.O. Burford (aged 38), a slaughterman. The latter received a conditional exemption. In Lawson's case, however, Lieutenant Wood said that 'it was necessary for the firm to prove that it was in the national interests that people should eat sausages and polonies (laughter)' and he was refused.

· Hill Paul and Co. appealed for two of their workers, W.P. Crosby (aged 30) and A.C. Gardner (aged 34). Both were employed as coat pressers engaged on government work, very much in arrears on account of shortage of labour. Crosby was passed fit for general service, with a delay of two months, Gardner for garrison duty at home.

· Stroud Co-op requested renewal of exemptions for five of its bakers, all passed fit for home duties. Lieutenant Wood admitted that the Society had a good case, and the men were exempted until 31 March.

The Urban and Rural Tribunal members dealt with similar claims every week as hundreds of local families realised the impact of losing their breadwinner, or businesses losing key workers and managers. Tempers frayed occasionally under the pressure of hard choices. On 5 May 1916, during an appeal by Hill Paul for a cutter needed to complete a military contract, Lieutenant Wood probably regretted his aside that 'the military authorities wished to put a stop to the vicious practice of appeals' although he accepted Mr Paul's word that there would be no further appeal. Mr Paul somewhat hotly retorted that he was not in the habit of saying what he did not mean.

INDUSTRY

The impact on Stroud's manufacturing industries was significant and, though some firms did well, not all were still trading in the 1920s. Stroud cloth had an enviable reputation worldwide and well before 1914 many local mills were providing high-quality cloth for military use. Every mill became involved in production for the war effort, although the *Stroud News* editor complained that Trowbridge's mills, working night and day, might send work Stroud's way!

Even the local flock mills – regarded with some disdain by the high-end cloth mill owners – came into their own. Shoddy and flock did not need modern buildings and equipment and so the mill owners carried on recycling old cloth to be re-woven for cheap suits (shoddy) and stuffing for mattresses and cheap pillows (flock). Now their shoddy was needed to make uniforms. Their raw material increased when they were required to recycle worn or damaged uniforms from the front. One elderly resident remembers seeing railway wagons at Woodchester station packed with blood-spattered khaki, although there was probably more mud than blood.

On 30 April 1915 the *Stroud News* summarised the current position in Stroud:

> The cloth mills are busy with khaki contracts, several engineering works have secured large munitions contracts, and there is very little unemployment in the district. While the output of khaki and navy for the British forces and of mustard cloth for Russia is at present not as great as it was a little time ago, the demands of the French Government for blue-grey army cloths are very considerable. In addition, many mills are now hard at work trying to make up the arrears lost through war contracts in the production of costume cloth. Not only have the requirements of this country to be met in the matter of civilian clothing, but with Lille, Roubaix and Elberfield out of the market at present the mills of Great Britain are the only manufactories of these goods in Europe.

A brief report in the *Stroud News* of 11 June 1915 shows that Apperly Curtis, for one, did not discontinue its Continental trade straight away. A case of cloth shipped to Constantinople had been stolen but the witnesses – the ship's captain and officers – were by then interned in Turkey. The judge found in favour of Apperly Curtis.

For the cloth mill managers, the war caused hold-ups and cancellations. Eastern Germany had been the source of fine merino wool in 1914; now it had to come all the way from Australia, avoiding German U-boats. Synthetic blue dye had only been available from Germany; now it had to be replaced by natural indigo, costing 50 per cent more and harder to work (Marling and Evans, fulfilling a contract for pale blue cloth for the French, temporarily turned the River Frome blue!). During 1915 Worth's carpet factory advertised for energetic girls for carpet weaving. Hill Paul advertised for trouser machinists and finishers,

Holloway's advertisement from 7 November 1914. (Courtesy of the Gloucestershire Echo)

Strachan's was recruiting boys and girls aged 14 and 15 to work at Lodgemore Mill, and Holloway's advertised for shirt machinists – experienced or learners.

The majority of British Army uniforms were made in the huge clothing factories around Leeds, but Stroud's weaving and clothing mills all received orders for khaki cloth or military clothing. Holloway's reported working overtime on overcoats. A War Office order to Hill Paul in October 1917 was for supply of specified garments for a period of seven weeks, under the 1914 Defence of the Realm Act (DORA) regulations. The cost of making up the garments was left to the manufacturer but had to comply with the new wage clause and be agreed in advance by the Director of Army Contracts.

All manufacturers had problems outside their control. The most instant was the number of staff who volunteered. Local recruits to Lord Kitchener's Army were sent to Horfield Barracks for processing and, in the first two weeks of the war, fifty men left Dudbridge Ironworks and forty-five from Stroud Brewery. Other industries soon found it hard to get raw materials but the skills of walking stick-makers and pin-makers were quickly diverted to war production.

Dudbridge Ironworks had secured a contract the previous March to make Salmson aeroplane engines, and switched all its staff and capacity to war work for the duration. During a visit by the Minister of Munitions in September 1914, a director of the Ironworks was pleased to announce that they had been asked to produce 16,000 shell caps and by mid-September the works was advertising for 'Apprentices in all Departments'. By March 1915 a manager told the *Stroud News* that they were already employed full-time on government work and if more was wanted then the government would have to supply more men. It seems Mr Lloyd George had brought some factories under direct government control without consulting him.

Erinoid was one Stroud company that prospered as a direct consequence of the war, expanding eventually to become BP Chemicals at Lightpill. In 1914 Erinoid suddenly became the main UK producer of casein-based plastic – essential for uniform buttons and fireproof military components. The Erinoid plant was set up by Ernest Petersen to replace a similar company (Syrolit) at Lightpill that had failed in 1912 because of German competition. Petersen had been headhunted from that German manufacturer after meeting a Syrolit director at a Paris exhibition in 1912, and was in Stroud by early 1914. He found new equipment, devised the production method and new trading name, and Erinoid was up and running as war broke out. Then – a great irony – Petersen and his family were confined to the works site 'for the duration' because he was an enemy alien. At the end of the war the company's chairman was proud to say that Erinoid plastic was 'now used in every battleship, tank, telephone, signalling lamp and aeroplane'.

Erinoid advertisement. (Courtesy of Grace's Guide*)*

Another successful company was T.H. & J. Daniels, whose engines and pumps already had a secure place before the Great War in local manufacturing and agricultural businesses. During the First World War, as well as armaments, they made portable water treatment equipment to provide drinking water for the troops; they also fitted out Erinoid, just down the hill, with its first hydraulic presses and extruders.

But the changed circumstances also caused business failures. One of the first was S. Smiths & Sons at Brimscombe Brewery, who called in the receivers within a year. In September 1915 their brewery plant and twenty-four pubs were

---

CHALFORD.

High Street.

DAVIS & CHAMPION

are instructed by Mr. H. O. Gardiner (who has joined His Majesty's Forces) TO SELL BY AUCTION, upon the premises,

On WEDNESDAY, JULY 5th, 1916, commencing punctually at One o'clock,

2 VERY STAUNCH CART HORSES; useful COB; 12 Strong STORE PIGS; SOW heavy in farrow; HEIFER; BULLOCK; 70 Head of POULTRY; 30 CHICKEN; TWO LORRIES, nearly new; Narrow-wheel TIP CART; Sets of Thiller, G.O., and Trap HARNESS; FOWL HOUSES and RUNS; Coops; WAGGON SHEETS; Quantity of WIRE NETTING; HURDLES; Pig Troughs; Wheelbarrow, Stable Tools and Utensils; Miscellaneous Effects, and a few lots of Household FURNITURE.

STROUD: THE CROSS.

CARTER & BROTHERIDGE

have been instructed by Mr. B. F. King, who is joining His Majesty's Forces, to SELL BY AUCTION, on the Premises,

On THURSDAY, 6th JULY, 1916, at 3 p.m. precisely,

THE whole of his

STOCK-IN-TRADE and EFFECTS,

comprising Two Shaving Chairs, Ladies' Gas Hair Drier, Machine Brushes and Fittings, Razors; Ladies' Pads, Combs & Slides; Shaving Brushes & various Soaps; Hair Brushes, Combs and Oils; Two Panel Mirrors, Six Bentwood Chairs; Set 8-tread Steps, Linoleum, and other Effects of the business of a Hairdresser.

For further particulars apply to the Auctioneers.

Auctioneers' Offices: 8 Rowcroft, Stroud.

This Stroud Journal *advertisement from 30 June 1916 shows two small traders selling their businesses because they had to go to war. (Courtesy of the* Stroud News and Journal*)* put up for auction. Immediately after the war, some businesses failed through loss of orders, or customers, or both. Dudbridge Ironworks and Newman Henders – having had to abandon civilian customers in favour of full-time government contracts – found it impossible to get them back and called in the receivers, though both companies were rescued at the last minute by local investors. The Hound Brand Works in Slad Road – the smallest of Stroud's ready-made clothing factories – went into liquidation on 10 October 1919. Between 1914 and 1923 the number of Stroud small traders fell by about 20 per cent.

Business failure, when it came, was not always immediate. Following the death on the battlefield in August 1916 of Arthur Apperly, the woollen manufacturer Apperly & Curtis slowly failed and the business was forced into liquidation in 1933 – just in time for Redlers to buy the site and set up its own successful business. Abdela & Mitchell, the Brimscombe steamboat builders, produced many Admiralty vessels between 1914 and 1919 and continued producing for overseas customers for a short time after the war, but orders dropped and the company closed after a fire in 1925.

WOMEN'S WORK

In September 1914 Mr Godsell, chairman of Stroud Urban District Council, held a meeting to raise interest in the formation of a local branch of the Queen's 'Work for Women' Fund, but very few people attended and as a consequence no action was taken. But then the women of Stroud, who for generations had quietly run households, kept accounts and organised church bazaars, stepped into the public arena of fundraising with enthusiasm and enterprise. Mrs Ida Hyett, chair of the local War Relief Committee's sub-committee for Women's Employment, used the *Stroud News* to appeal for support for the number of women now short of work. While certain industries (notably cloth weaving) were busier than usual, many others (pin making, carpet and silk weaving, and tailoring) were working short time, causing considerable hardship to the families involved. The sub-committee organised home knitting and sewing work for these women who, Mrs Hyett was pleased to say, had already made 265 body belts, thirty-six mufflers and forty-eight pairs of socks for the troops. (One knitting pattern carried the stern warning 'only an experienced knitter should undertake this sock'!)

The *Stroud News* of 5 October 1917 reported that the Holy Trinity Parish Knitting Party, in Stroud, had completed 1,179 different articles of wear, including over 600 pairs of socks. Miss Clissold asked for parcels of old clothes, fit for remaking for local relief, to be left for her at the Labour Exchange on Lansdown.

Another young woman persuaded the Red Cross to deliver crates of donated eggs to the front. Practical help was being organised locally, and the women were doing it.

One local young woman was more than ready to experience freedom. Selsley vicar's daughter Mary Gabrielle West quickly volunteered to work in a Red Cross hospital in Cheltenham, even though she had – as she later told a BBC interviewer – 'only been trained to run a household'. From there she became a canteen supervisor and within a year was in charge of the nightshift kitchens at Woolwich Arsenal munitions works. She had a special dispensation from the dog-loving Assistant Lady Superintendent to have her terrier with her on night duty. Miss West then joined the new Women's Police Service and spent the rest of the war as a sergeant, supervising female workers in munitions factories. Miss West recorded in her diary that these mostly city-born working-class women used language seldom heard in Selsley!

In 1915 gathering the harvest was a problem and a letter printed in March 1915 suggested that although few women could handle a scythe, or drive a cutting machine, they could turn the hay, drive carts, and throw the hay up for a man to build the rick.

> There would be plenty of women to gather in the hay if the farmers' wives and daughters were not too grand nowadays to work themselves … Ladies of well-known local position are needed to lead the way, and show that 'noblesse oblige' by working themselves.

The writer of this letter, Mr M.H. Mason – late Senior Inspector for the Local Government Board – was clearly finding retirement irksome.

The opportunity for women to work brought an unexpected benefit. In an era where ordinary families rented their homes, one Stroud couple took on a mortgage, paid from the wife's earnings. They had never dreamt of owning their home but one of their granddaughters today lives in the same house on the side of Rodborough Common.

The Women's Land Army, formed in 1917, provided half of all farm labour by the end of the war. Evelyn Pollard's reminiscence of life in Randwick includes this story, told to her by W. Stevens:

> We made a tremendous big hayrick at Rectory Farm and the government commandeered that one and another down the road. A group of soldiers brought the traction engine and the baler. They screwed the baler up too tight and burst the machine and it was idle for two or three weeks. What we had to do was to haul the

bales of hay down with horses and put them on the trucks to Stroud railway station. It went abroad, the baled hay, out to France, 'cos they had horses on the guns and everything. (From *Randwick and Roundabout* by Evelyn Pollard, 1986, p. 53)

Those whose position in society (or that of their husbands) would not allow them to work for a living organised bazaars, tea parties, children's entertainments and musical evenings, as well as being involved in social work, running small charities, or the local branches of national charities, and organising the long-term logistics of collecting and distributing significant sums of money or gifts for the front. Mrs Reginald Green (Mabel, the wife of Stroud's Medical Officer of Health) of Stratford Lawn, Cainscross, collected gifts of fruit and vegetables each Thursday to be sent to the Fleet. During one month alone 596lbs of produce was received from residents of the district.

The newspaper editors carefully published long lists that itemised every gift made and the name of the giver. The thoughtfulness of the presents is significant. Here is a summary of just one week's gifts to Standish Hospital in September 1915 by sixty-four individuals, two shops and two schools: eleven cakes, one handkerchief, thirty bags of vegetables and fruit, one jar of pickles, eleven boxes of eggs, two packs of butter, three jars of jam, four packs of cigarettes, one box of books, soap, an air cushion, tray cloths, and dish covers. Mrs Attwood donated 4*d* as well as her vegetables, and Selsley Sunday school children sent £1 15*s*.

Two young girls from Ebley, Norrie Carter (aged 12) and Ida Olpin (aged 11), made patchwork pincushions and kettle holders out of scrap cloth donated by local firms, and sold them very successfully in support of the Prince of Wales' National Relief Fund. During the summer term of 1916 boys at the Stroud and District Craft School made a number of articles for the military hospitals, including bed rests and bed tables, for the Belgravia Depot at Stroud.

EVERYDAY LIFE

Despite the individual fears and losses experienced by many, they kept their grief private. It was felt that the British people were strong enough to weather this distant horror so the correct outcome – victory – was inevitable and it was acceptable to pretend to ignore it in public.

One pleasing diversion in 1916 was the purchase of Stroud's empty Royal George Hotel by Mr Vincent Lawson, a Cirencester civil engineer and architect. Mr Lawson's plans for the new King Street Buildings included a restaurant, superior lock-up shops and discreet public lavatories. The *Stroud News* devoted a whole page to the project, explaining that there would be:

A NEW CUPID.

QUITE disheartened and sad, little Cupid
    Sat down 'mid the roses and sighed;
Looking dazed, and in fact, rather stupid,
For failure had wounded his pride.
He had wooed with the same winning graces,
And tempted with old witching wiles;
But the dark frowns he saw on all faces
Had banished his own sunny smiles.

What has come to our maidens, he queried,
Has Cupid no charm for them now?
And he busied his brain 'till 'twas wearied;
He knew he must conquer—but how?
Is the world growing colder, and changing?
Then Cupid must change too, he cried,
So forthwith he commenced re-arranging
The quiver of darts at his side.

With a wise, saucy look he departed,
He'd got an idea—so he said,
And was looking quite gay and light-hearted
As from the rose garden he sped.
And the very next time he went wooing
He wore a new garb, so they say;
So young maidens take care what you're doing
For Cupid's in Khaki to-day.

PHŒBE COLES,
Stroud, Glos.

Proceeds of sale will be devoted to the
British Red Cross Society (Central Fund)

*Mrs Phoebe Coles wrote this poem and the postcard was a steady fundraiser for the Red Cross hospital.
(Courtesy of Howard Beard)*

...a first-class restaurant and café on the first floor with a gentlemen's smoking room, and a ladies' lounge, provided with daily papers and writing accommodation, where friends can meet and wait luncheon and tea appointments, and customers can leave their parcels when shopping. Dinner parties, suppers and balls will also be catered for on the premises. Ladies' and gentlemen's toilet rooms, fitted with hot and cold water services, will also be provided, thus affording accommodation of such a nature that has never been provided before, and will supply a long felt want to the ever increasing number of visitors and motorists who pass through the town. (*Stroud News*, 7 January 1916)

Crucial to Mr Lawson's success was that a huge corner shop nearby had been taken by Hepworth's – a national tailoring chain whose advertisements in subsequent weeks must have infuriated Hill Paul and Holloway's, both struggling to keep government contracts going alongside their civilian output. Their quarter-

Hepworth's advertisement. (Courtesy of the Stroud News and Journal*)*

page advert in the *Stroud News* on 31 March 1916 shows the new block with the renovated Royal George and King Street Buildings – and their competitive prices.

Mr Lawson had also arranged the arrival to Stroud of F.W. Woolworth & Co., near Bath Street. The local newspaper reporter was fascinated with the idea of having a shop where nothing cost more than 6*d* and customers were expected to carry away their purchases themselves – a most novel idea:

> Never in the history of Stroud has a new business venture been launched amid
> more excitement and success. On Friday the spacious shop with its varied contents
> was thrown open to inspection ... Throughout the day people poured through the
> doors and, to give eclât to the occasion, a Band discoursed bright music ... Early
> on Saturday King Street, High Street and Rowcroft presented an unusual appear-
> ance, for people who had made purchases of pails and other hardware articles had
> to get them home, and goods which the previous day had been on view under a
> roof were now in evidence beneath the blue sky.

CINEMA

Radio broadcasting did not start until after the war and the only sources of news were newspapers and the cinema. The 'moving pictures' had just arrived in Stroud – the Empire Theatre in London Road offered twice-nightly pro-grammes and the Picture House on King Street included afternoon tea for its Circle Lounge patrons. A week's programme included live entertainment by local performers – songs, short plays, comics of the music hall variety – in addi-tion to the movies. The programme changed every week but always included a Pathé newsreel. After the newsreel there would be a short comic film (often American) then the main feature – usually just over an hour long, and silent, of course.

By 1917 the Picture House was changing its programme twice a week, as Hollywood got into its stride and churned out hundreds of comedies, romances, dramatic adventures, patriotic propaganda and stirring (but fictional) war hero-ics. In October 1916 the Empire Theatre proudly announced that it would be showing the film *The Battle of the Somme* – made for the British Government by two official reporters with the primary intention of sending it to the United States to persuade them into joining the war.

The Picture House opening programme from 8 December 1916. (Courtesy of the Stroud News *and* Journal*)*

ELSIE CHAMBERS

Born in Chalford in 1888, Elsie Chambers was to become a famous professional contralto. She was living in London when war broke out but soon joined Lena Ashwell's concert party, entertaining soldiers in camps behind the lines. Her lovely voice, and her ability to play the piano, made her services invaluable. She was also glad she had heeded Princess Victoria's advice to wear strong boots because she had to climb onto heavy lorries and walk through lots of mud.

Miss Chambers' father, a Territorial, was serving with the Glosters in Colchester but he got special leave for a home visit and was able to wave Elsie off from Stroud station when she left for France for the first time. (Of interest, Staff Sergeant Chambers was responsible for the gun carriage that carried Nurse Edith Cavell to

A studio portrait of Elsie Chambers. (Courtesy of Stroud Local History Society)

her funeral when her body was returned from France after the war. The band had been told to play only the first part of the Funeral March – a slow piece to match the required pace of the horses. Unfortunately, they then played the quicker second part. The horses sped up in response and Sergeant Chambers saw that the coffin was slipping very slowly from the gun carriage. He grabbed the lead horse and shouted to the band to repeat the first part until they arrived at the cemetery with dignity.)

Every year Miss Chambers organised a fundraising concert in Stroud – and on one return visit brought a message to the family of a soldier she had met whilst singing in France. Her songs ranged from opera to music hall and she brought her friends to sing along, as well as inviting local performers to take part. Special late trains and buses were laid on to take the humming audiences home to the surrounding villages. The *Stroud News* of 12 February 1916 reported:

> Miss Elsie Chambers' patriotic concert, which was given in the Subscription Rooms, Stroud, last (Thursday) evening, was undoubtedly the most successful she has ever given in Stroud. The proceeds were in aid of the Lord Lieutenant's County Relief Fund for Gloucestershire.

The following month she was back in France. At her 1917 concert she sang an additional verse to the national anthem, which no doubt brought tears to many in the audience:

> *God bless our splendid men.*
> *Bring them safe home again; God bless our men.*
> *Make them victorious, patient, chivalrous –*
> *They are so dear to us; God save our men.*

In 1918, on a street in Cologne, she was hailed by a despatch rider – her cousin Stanley Evans from Brimscombe. Both were extremely relieved to see each other.

AUSTRALIAN ENTERTAINERS

The Australian Flying Corps, stationed at Minchinhampton Aerodrome, entertained Stroud and the wider area with their 'While the Billy Boils' show.

In June 1917 the *Stroud News* printed an ecstatic review, describing how the curtain rose on a swagman, a tramp, a cook, an overseer, a boundary rider and a wandering violinist in the Australian Bush, and the evening took off from there. The three-hour-long entertainment included songs, recitations and jokes; the audience was convulsed with laughter and there was not a dull moment. So many people had been unable to get tickets that the Australians agreed to come back the following night and do it all again. And they did, raising substantial funds for the Red Cross and the Belgravia War Supply Depot at Far Hill.

These young men were trainee pilots and were well known for their daft behaviour: they flew low over the town, sang loudly and inappropriately, flirted with the girls, and noisily alarmed the residents of Tetbury, where many of them were billeted. Their show must have been very refreshing for the war-tired residents of the Stroud district, and bitter-sweet for many. One Australian stayed on after the war and founded the Red Bus Company – one of the first public bus services in Stroud, providing regular routes around the county. Elsie Chambers' younger sister Zoura was employed to help in the office.

SKATING IN THE PARK – MRS GREEN CLEANS UP

The unusually cold winter of 1916/17 brought one piece of serendipity for the people of Stroud, when the lake at Stratford Park froze over. Mrs Mabel Green (the collector of fruit and vegetables for the navy) took advantage of the snow, and the many visitors to the park:

With helpers galore she arranged for the ice surface to be kept clean so that the skaters were able to glide with ease and comfort in the pale moonlight. She also took good care that nimble pence were extracted from the pockets of those who availed themselves of the pleasure. The result was that everyone was delighted, and a nice little sum was netted for the fund in which Mrs Green is so keenly interested.

FOOD SHORTAGES

Bad weather, poor harvests, loss of shipping to German submarines, and the need to supply soldiers at the front greatly reduced the amount of food available in the shops as the war went on. The prices of locally produced food came as a shock to housewives who, before the war, had happily bought Free Trade food imported at the lowest possible price. By mid-January 1915 the *Stroud News* reported a 20 per cent rise in the cost of food since the war had started four months previously. It pointed out that before the war three-quarters of Stroud's families only just got by, with little or nothing left at the end of the week. Compared with the year before when prices seemed high, the price of beef was 12 per cent higher, bacon and butter 10 per cent, eggs 33 per cent, sugar 50 per cent, and beer was now not only in short supply, but now being taxed at 25 per cent of its former price. It was a blessing that the cloth mills were all busy with army orders.

Despite the enforced drop in imports the government was reluctant to introduce any form of official rationing and for the first few years of the war shopkeepers sold what they could, though the government imposed fixed prices. Early in 1915, the President of the Board of Trade suggested that if every person ate 2lb of meat less per month, supplies would be sufficient. Compared with 1914, the cost of meat had doubled whilst the cost of vegetables had halved. Buying (and eating) English fruit and vegetables made economic sense as well as contributing to the war effort. The local paper reported: 'In society circles, a vogue for vegetarian food had a marked effect upon high-class cuisine', but it probably did not impact greatly on sales at Stroud's pie and faggot shops.

THE PATRIOTIC ECONOMY EXHIBITION

The Patriotic Economy Exhibition was another of Mabel Green's good ideas. After a great deal of backroom planning, Countess Bathurst opened the exhibition at the Stroud Subscription Rooms on 26 May 1917. The *Stroud News* reported:

His Majesty the King was asking them to do a difficult task – to build up the bodies of the children and keep themselves fit and in good working condition on a diet where meat, bread and potatoes should be reduced to the smallest possible proportions. This exhibition was going to teach them how. There would be a competition for the best meatless dinner without potatoes and bread (laughter).

Lady Bathurst went on to suggest that well-to-do people could easily manage on 2lbs of flour and bread a week, and if the working class adhered to Lord Devonport's rations (the Minister of Food recommended 4lbs a week) she did not think there would be any cause for anxiety. And she was pleased to announce that the United States of America was sending a very large consignment of sugar for jam-making in the home, so that they would not after all have to make sugarless jam.

The week-long exhibition, reported in exhaustive detail in the *Stroud News* of 1 June 1917 (which included every stall holder, every helper, every organiser), contained stalls and offered leaflets about a surprising variety of subjects: bees, domestic economy, glove waistcoats (an ingenious way of re-stitching old kid gloves into light, windproof garments), infant welfare, handicrafts by wounded soldiers, home contrivances, literature, wheat flour substitutes, war hospital supply depots, war savings, and the salvage of waste paper and waste metal and tinfoil (the sale of which had raised several hundred pounds).

Mr Paddison, the Propagandist for the Stroud and Nailsworth areas of the Food Control Campaign, worked 'like a Trojan' all week according to the *Stroud News*. Hour after hour he explained the recipe for, and benefit of, baking Cornish pasties, admirably suited for workmen or children who took their meals away from home.

There were demonstrations of gardening, tools, electrical cooking and heating, gas cookers and water boilers, and competitions, including one for under-14s for useful items made from scrap material. There were free lectures on 'Growing Potatoes', 'Milk from Goats', 'Cheese-making', 'Infant Welfare', 'Caring for your Teeth', and evening cookery demonstrations. All week on the green in front of the Subscription Rooms there were goats, rabbits and chickens – 'It is a veritable zoo,' said one bemused bystander. The final talk (suitably after the bedtime of small children) was by Mr Critchley, who had been responsible for the rabbit display all week. His demonstration had the sinister title 'Rabbits for Utility Purposes', although whether this involved rabbit pies baked in one of the new modern domestic ovens the newspaper did not say. Overall, the exhibition was a huge success and 'one of the most comprehensive and successful of its kind ever held'.

Rationing was finally introduced in early 1918 for tea, meat, butter and sugar, and residents had to register with one shopkeeper for each item. Local Food Committees implemented the system, and Mr Philip Ford, chairman of Stroud's Food Control committee, was praised in the *Stroud News* for his sensible management and clear explanation of how it would function. However, the system did not work quite so well in its first week, when the Food Control office only allowed shopkeepers to supply 2oz of butter per person per week, instead of the announced 4oz, without any forewarning. The result was 'a good deal of complaint' in the shops.

On one occasion, after Gloucester Market had allocated six sheep for the Stroud district, the imminent meat shortage was quickly solved by Stroud's two Co-op Society butchers making a quick but discreet visit to three Bisley farms, requisitioning forty-five sheep and distributing them to the town's butcher shops – local knowledge and familiarity with the farmers bent the rules but saved everyone's tempers.

THE FLOUR SHORTAGE

Mr Tuck, baker of Gloucester Street, invented new recipes and advertised that he now sold Barley Bread, scones containing only 25 per cent of wheat flour, and cakes and biscuits containing no wheat flour at all and sweetened without sugar – all at moderate prices – as his contribution to 'Patriotic Economy'. Many customers thought brown bread was only good enough for poor people, but everyone had to get used to the bakers' ingenuity in managing without flour.

BEER

There was real concern in society about excessive drinking. There were Temperance Societies in most towns, including Stroud – there was even a temperance hotel on Rowcroft, and another on Russell Street. To begin with, the government tried to control drinking by putting up the duty on beer and spirits. Salmon Springs Brewery responded in December 1914 with an advert pointing out that since the government now charged 23s tax on every barrel, customers would be actively helping the war effort by sticking to their pre-war consumption. The editor of the *Stroud News* wrote a carefully worded column that managed to express concern for the local breweries as businesses while at the same time saying how pleased the temperance societies would be.

In 1915 the government doubled the duty on spirits and quadrupled wine duty to raise an extra £1.5 million. A supplementary tax on strong beers was expected to yield £1.6 million and the limit on national output was reduced to 10 million barrels compared to the previous 36 million. Stroud's breweries were hard hit – not only had they to reduce their output, they had to find customers prepared to pay the huge increase in prices. By 1918 the cost of materials for making beer had more than doubled; the cost of horse fodder nearly doubled (if they still had any horses), brewery wages increased, and the cost of a gallon of petrol (if they still had any wagons) had trebled to 3s. The consequence of all this was that a refreshing drink of beer at the end of a long working day was suddenly more expensive than whisky. Many actually switched to whisky, which was not the plan at all.

LOCAL INVENTIONS RESULTING FROM THE WAR

Harry Baughan – whose retired parents had come to live in Stroud – was called up but found unfit for active service, so he was promoted to corporal and made responsible for catering logistics at his army camp. He quickly became aware of the problems of moving motorised transport – especially despatch riders' motorbikes – over uneven and muddy terrain and started to explore possible mechanical solutions. Later he designed and demonstrated a new type of differential to the army on their tank ranges. Harry's ingenious and robust designs transformed the performance of sidecars and two-seater cycle-cars. He was soon winning races and competitions with cars made at his workshop at Piccadilly Mills in Stroud, using the Nailsworth Ladder as a testing ground.

Redler's was a small company operating at Sharpness Docks, moving flour from ships into silos and then into bags. It was essential that the flour be kept moving. When wartime staff shortages meant the nightshift could no longer run, the flour settled and compacted in the hoppers. Arnold Redler invented a method of breaking it loose. He patented his continuous chain as the en masse bulk flow handling system that became the principle of all his later conveyor systems, and a worldwide business, and in 1933 moved to premises in Stroud.

Sandwich degree courses were first introduced by Bristol University in 1916, as a way of training professional engineers. Wallers, at the Phoenix Iron Works in Thrupp, and Lister's in Dursley were two of the first companies to work with the university in providing the practical experience that formed part of the degree qualification.

TNT

In August 1918 the *Stroud News* reported on an unusual reward:

> Mr E N Marchant of Bath Road, Stroud, was the recipient of a special reward from the Inventions Board of the Ministry of Munitions in recognition of services rendered in an important improvement in the manufacture of the high explosive TNT.

This might be connected to one of the oddest requests of the war: a War Office notice circulated round local schools and youth organisations offering children 7s 6d for every hundredweight of conkers they could take to their local railway station. Some 3,000 tonnes of conkers (about 60,000cwt) were collected and transported to the Synthetic Products Company at King's Lynn, where they were used to make acetone, a vital component of the smokeless propellant for shells and bullets known as cordite. On 9 November 1917, the *Stroud News* reported that, 'The children of Leonard Stanley collected one ton of horse chestnuts for the Ministry of Munitions.' None of the children knew why they were doing it, but it was an exciting addition to the autumn school timetable.

RED CROSS AND VAD HOSPITALS

Across the country, county-level branches of the Red Cross had made plans to provide temporary hospitals in the event of war, and to provide equipment and nursing staff. In the Stroud district three buildings were made ready – Standish House north of Stonehouse (lent for the duration by Lord Sherborne), Chestnut House in Nailsworth (earlier the home of the Clissold brewery family) and the Rooms of Holy Trinity church (across the road from Stroud General Hospital and lent by the Revd Hawkins).

The War Office paid grants to hospitals for every patient they looked after, and the amount increased annually during the war. At the highest rate, the government paid £1 4s 6d per week, or £63 14s 0d per annum, for each patient. This covered full hospital treatment, food and other costs. The official food allowances were generously augmented by local donations, in cash and in kind, as local fundraising started to take off. Fresh fruit and vegetables were regularly left in the kitchens, and the *Stroud News* celebrated the record set in April 1917 by Mrs H.E. Trinder of George Street, who had collected and donated 1,000 eggs for the patients at the Trinity Rooms and Roxborough House.

The head of the Gloucestershire division of the Red Cross was Captain Maynard Francis Colchester-Wemyss, son of the chairman of Stroud Brewery, whose family home was at Westbury Court. His full-time Assistant Director was Miss Clementina Dorothy Allen of Southfields, Woodchester. By 1917 Miss Allen had learned to use a slide rule, reducing the time spent on the accounts from three days to one hour!

The Stroud Red Cross had been set up by the Caruthers-Little family at Edge in 1910. One of the main supporters was Mrs Caines Terry. In 1913 she and Miss Allen went to a national training centre in Hatfield and brought back the practices and methods that were then used in Gloucestershire. The most important was the idea of casualty simulation – practising with real people instead of dummies, which the Stroud Red Cross carried out with the Gloucestershire Yeomanry in preparation for any possible invasion (the modern Casualties Union was an offshoot of this early training method).

By the time war was declared Gloucestershire was prepared and, by 1916, the county had twenty-two VAD hospitals and 2,200 beds. Nationally the Red Cross provided 50,000 beds of which Gloucestershire provided 4 per cent, more than double its proportionate share, and the county came second only to Lancashire in its provision. Local volunteers were organised into groups, called Voluntary Aid Detachments (VADs). The ideal organisational set-up for a Detachment was defined as fifty men, twenty-five women (one of whom should be a trained nurse), a doctor, a pharmacist and four cooks. Nearly 95 per cent of the 2,000 workers in Gloucestershire Red Cross Hospitals during the Great War gave their services freely, many coming in after their normal work.

There were seven Women's Detachments in the Stroud district and their commandants and quartermasters were all local wives or daughters of what had in Victorian times been called the Great and Good: Chalford had Mrs Whybrow of Skaiteshill House and Mrs Edwards of The Corderies; Minchinhampton had Miss Grist of Hillfield and Mrs James of La Bicoque; Nailsworth had Mrs Martin of Millbrook and Miss Skrine of Horsley Court; Painswick had Miss M. Hyett of Painswick House and Miss Caruthers-Little of Pitchcombe House, Stonehouse had Miss Meyrick-Jones of Stanley House and Miss Phillimore, and Woodchester had Mrs Huth of The Achers and Miss C. Allen of Southfield.

The person in charge of Stroud's Detachment – the Commandant – was Mrs Louisa Margaret Martin (wife of Stroud's Medical Officer of Health, whose home was at The Chestnuts at the top of Hollow Lane). She filled the role at the Trinity Rooms for the duration of the war. Her Quartermaster was Miss Ada Mary James, of Frome Hall. The Men's Detachment Commandant was Mr Watson Benjamin Evans.

On 30 October 1914 the *Stroud News* reported the following:

Soldiers arrive in Stroud

At about 6 o'clock on Wednesday over twenty soldiers – British and Belgian – arrived in Stroud, having been brought from Bristol Infirmary, where they have recovered from the more serious effects of their wounds, to make room for further cases arriving daily from the front. As on the occasion when the Belgian refugees were brought to Stroud, the townspeople turned out in their hundreds – nay, thousands – to welcome the newcomers and the thoroughfares near the railway stations (GWR and Midland) were crowded with spectators. On arrival in the town, the soldiers, whose wounds were of a varied nature, were assisted from the railway carriages into the conveyances which in turn drew up at the kerb, and their appearance was the signal for outbursts of tremendous cheering.

There was much handshaking and a special welcome for a soldier well enough to emerge on a crutch. Tommy Reed, a well-known Stroud motoring pioneer, was among those who provided transport for the troops and also collected bedding and other necessities. Ten soldiers were accommodated at the General Hospital, the remainder at the Trinity Rooms where 'roaring fires slowly toasted the men who reposed comfortably before them in big armchairs, while fourteen beds, each with a night-shirt and screens, are arranged around the walls.'

Although the hospitals were partly funded by the government, fundraising events continued throughout the war; local people and traders were generous and constant in their support. Hundreds of pounds were donated from concerts, bazaars, and staff collections. The nation's farmers were particularly active – for the year ending December 1916 the county received the enormous sum of £5,085 as its share of proceeds raised by the British Farmers' Red Cross Society. The year before, Sandoe & Sons had held a fruit sale and donated 8s 6d. On several occasions the local press published detailed lists of gifts sent in for local VAD hospitals. In November 1914, for instance, Mr Aiken-Sneath gave thirteen brace of pheasants. Other gifts ranged from blancmange to slippers! Lady Apperly sent some Irish stew, while Uplands Sunday school constructed what was described as a 'dressing wagon' for the ward. In the spring of 1917 Standish VAD hospital received from a Berkeley working party twenty-three flannel vests, fourteen handkerchiefs and a hotwater bottle cover.

This was the Commandant Mrs Martin's description of the Trinity Rooms' Red Cross hospital:

The Stroud Red Cross Hospital at its commencement had provision for 30 beds, 20 in Trinity Parish Rooms, lent by the Vicar of the parish, and 10 in the General Hospital a few yards away. The proximity of the hospital to Trinity Rooms made the nursing and care of seriously wounded soldiers possible, for while the Trinity Rooms provided a lofty, light, well ventilated building with class rooms for office, bath room and store room, there was no available place for operating theatre and X-ray room, etc. One small class room was fitted up as a surgery, but was unsuitable for undertaking operations. A small lean-to office was built at the Trinity Rooms. The kitchen itself was an adapted 'lean-to', in which it was wonderful that such excellent cooking was done. In 1916 60 further beds were provided, partly in Roxborough House, kindly lent by the Stroud Board of Guardians, and partly by giving up the room hitherto used as an office, and also by the setting aside of five further beds at the General Hospital, making a total accommodation of 90 beds.

The Trinity Rooms Admissions Register, a rare surviving document, shows that the patients belonged to regiments from across the country. Of more than 1,000 treated, only thirty were from the Glosters and there were thirteen Canadians, two Australians and fourteen Belgians. Until Standish opened, convalescent beds were provided at the Red Cross hospital at Chestnut Hill House in Nailsworth – their names too survived, as did some of their autographs, in a book found in the 1970s by Howard Beard in a local junk shop.

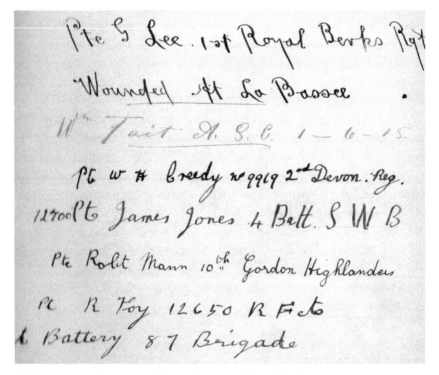

Soldiers' signatures in an autograph book. (Courtesy of Howard Beard)

Soldiers recuperating at the Trinity Rooms were not, it would seem, totally confined to barracks. In April 1915 a certain Albert Hadlow was charged with being drunk and disorderly in Badbrook and with assaulting PC Phillips. Hadlow and another Red Cross hospital patient 'were both throwing their caps at one another' when PC Phillips told them to go back to the Trinity Rooms and set off up the hill with them. Outside the Mason's Arms, PC Phillips was struck by Hadlow who then 'divested himself of his coat and tunic' – clearly ready for a proper fight – and PC Phillips reluctantly had to arrest him and take him back down to the police station.

THE ARMISTICE

The 11 November Armistice was signalled at 11 a.m. by the clanging of the bell on Holloway's factory; mill sirens hooted and within minutes the streets were filled with 'excited citizens and bright faced, never-may-care schoolchildren'. Drapers sold tricolour ribbon, quickly made into bows and rosettes, and everybody was 'gaily bedecked'.

A public service of thanksgiving was held at the parish church (where Stanley Evans, home on leave, played the organ). In the afternoon a parade through the town included District Councillors, the Men's VAD Detachment, wounded soldiers, munitions workers, motor cars, motorbikes and carriages carrying the flags of the Allies. The Australian airmen arrived from Minchinhampton, cheering and 'making things hum'. At the Subscription Rooms the Gloucestershire Volunteer Regiment fired blank rounds into the air, accompanied by bugles and the rolling of drums, followed by many speeches. The Town Band played in King Street Parade and everyone sang along. Street celebrations continued into the evening, with a peripatetic display of fireworks and Verey lights – 'a not-to-be-forgotten night'.

With great relief, and dreadful regrets, the people of Stroud resumed normal life. The war had brought many changes and peace had come at a great price.

2
STROUD'S VICTORIA CROSS

LIEUTENANT EUGENE PAUL BENNETT VC, MC

STEVE PITMAN

The Victoria Cross (VC) is the highest military decoration awarded for valour 'in the face of the enemy' to members of the armed forces of Britain and most Commonwealth countries plus previous British Empire territories. During the Great War a total of 628 VCs were awarded and one, in November 1916, was won by a soldier who was born and grew up in Stroud.

Eugene Paul Bennett (known to family and friends simply as Paul) attended Marling School then moved from the family home in Rodborough to London in 1910, where he became a clerk in the Bank of England. Perhaps this job was not exciting enough because it didn't last long and in October 1913 he joined the 28th County of London Battalion (Artists Rifles) as Private No. 1253, with whom he was mobilised at the outbreak of the Great War, entering France on 19 October 1914.

Captain Eugene Paul Bennett VC, MC. (© S&N Genealogy Supplies, with permission)

Consequently, Private Bennett had the good fortune to witness one of the rare happy events of the war – the 1914 Christmas Truce – when in many (but by no means all) trench sectors on the Western Front both sides laid down their weapons and called a temporary, unofficial truce for forty-eight hours or so and fraternised with the enemy. Events varied from sector to sector but in most it began on Christmas Eve with carol singing on both sides for the entertainment of the other. By Christmas morning this had developed in most places into the enemies congregating together in No Man's Land, some just chatting, lots playing football, others exchanging barrels of German beer for British plum puddings or tunic buttons or tobacco. One officer later wrote: 'I awoke at dawn and on emerging on all fours from my dugout, became aware that the trench was practically empty. I stood upright in the mud and looked over the parapet. No Man's Land was full of clusters ... of khaki and grey ... pleasantly chatting together.' On Boxing Day, however, the generals of both sides regained control and the men were ordered to be enemies again rather than friends.

Paul Bennett wrote a letter home to his father on that Boxing Day, saying that he had spent a most 'enjoyable Christmas' with an 'amnesty along the line from 7 a.m. Both sides stood above their trenches and exchanged tobacco and shouted greetings.' Following the truce things soon returned to normal, however, and he continued with less pleasant news:

> ... back to trenches ... heavy 24 hrs ... rather a nightmare ... dark ... mud very deep ... sharp crackle of rifles ... soft hiss of bullets ... magnesium flares ... horse whisper to keep absolutely still ... takes an hour to move a mile ... back bent double ... sat in the mud with our backs against the trench ... 4 casualties ... helped bury 2 of them, in doing which we unearthed a buried German. I ate no more food after that ... I was not sorry to get out the next night in spite of the nine miles' march to the billets. Thank the mater ... ripping parcel ... we are having snow & sleet ... very cold ... am afraid this war will be longer than people at first thought ... Germans are no mean foe!

Soon after, on 30 December 1914, he gained a commission with the 2nd Battalion Worcestershire Regiment as a Second Lieutenant and joined them on 16 January at Gorre in northern France, near Bethune. During 1915 he was in front line action with his regiment at the Battle of Festubert in February and again in September at the disastrous Battle of Loos (the first 'Big Push') where British casualty numbers were an enormous 61,000, many falling victim to their own release of poison gas when the wind changed direction and blew it straight back at them.

On 26 September, the second day of the battle, Bennett took part in his battalion's attack near La Bassée. The battalion war diary states that late in the afternoon they

> advanced magnificently at a steady double until the front German trench was reached [which] almost without halting was leaped by the successive lines [of soldiers] who still went bravely forward towards the trenches occupied by the enemy who had now opened rapid rifle and machine gun fire on the advancing lines and casualties were numerous but still the advance continued until an old German half-dug trench was reached where the front line took what little cover the parapet afforded and opened fire on the German trench about 200 yards in front.

Although a partially successful assault, the diary continues 'our losses were found to be severe, no less than 13 officers being killed and wounded … and 300 other ranks. All the officers of B company were wounded.' Despite their efforts and suffering, they were not relieved from the front line or allowed to march back to billets for a further four days. The diary continued: 'having tea with rum and bread and cheese en route. This was very much appreciated by the men in their exhausted state and being the only hot drink in five days. Billets were reached between 8:00 am & 9:00 am and the remainder of the day was spent in sleep'.

The first of Paul Bennett's bravery awards came about on 10 November 1915, when he and his 2nd Battalion were moved into front line trenches near the village of Cambrin. Officers and men were just settling down in their new position in the evening's fading light when a huge explosion shattered their trenches. The Germans had detonated an underground mine just in front of their line and about 70 yards of front trenches were destroyed. As the flying debris settled back down to earth, the Germans lit up the scene with a large searchlight and raked the entire area with machine-gun fire. The explosion had buried many men. Some had totally disappeared, while others were buried up to their necks or waists in the mud. Second Lieutenant Bennett led rescue parties over the debris to dig out the trapped survivors, the whole area illuminated by the German searchlight and under machine gun fire from just 30 yards away. They continued digging until all the survivors were freed but a bombing battle for the possession of the crater ensued, which lasted all night. By dawn, however, the crater had been secured by the Worcesters and the sector was quiet. Five soldiers had died and a further twenty-three were hospitalised with shock and wounds. For his bravery in this action Second Lieutenant E.P. Bennett was awarded the Military Cross, which he received at Buckingham Palace from King George V on 10 May 1916. His parents travelled up from Rodborough to be present at the event.

In July 1916 the 2nd Worcesters were moved to the Somme to be part of the next 'Big Push', a battle which was intended to be the big breakthrough but instead became one of the bloodiest battles in human history, with 20,000 British deaths on the first day alone. Successes were few, small and very costly on the Somme and in November 1916 Paul Bennett's battalion took part in the three-day attack at the Transloy Ridges in the east of the region. It was just a minor engagement in the scale of things that summer and autumn, but highly significant for him and those around him. The weather for weeks had been cold and wet, leaving the ground – in the words of General Haig – 'sodden with rain and broken up everywhere by innumerable shell-holes, [and] can only be described as a morass, almost bottomless in places: between the lines and for many thousands of yards behind them it is almost – and in some localities, quite – impassable.' To make matters worse, as the 300 or so Worcesters (mostly newly arrived young soldiers) crouched in their muddy, shallow trenches at daybreak on 5 November, just before their advance was to begin, an enemy aeroplane spotted them from above, only yards from the German trenches and directed fierce artillery shellfire right onto them for hours, causing massive casualties including nearly all the officers and NCOs of 'D' Company, who were to be the first wave of the attack.

When the advance started they were immersed in an even greater barrage of shell and machine-gun fire but all four companies moved slowly forwards. Paul Bennett was struck by a shell fragment and while his wounds were being dressed he was surrounded by other wounded men in the shelter of a sunken lane and watched the last two companies move on through the fire. However, ahead of him, as the smoke of battle cleared briefly, he could see that the advance had stopped. The leading wave of bewildered young soldiers, many of whom were in their first action, having lost all their officers in the murderous fire, dropped to the ground for shelter. The following three waves caught up with them and also stopped, out in the open. A wounded sergeant crawled out of the sunken lane to lead them forwards but was immediately hit and fell. Paul Bennett, also in the sunken lane, grabbed a spade and cut some steps up the steep embankment before he too rushed forward, still grasping the spade, to the head of the stationary troops and signalled for them to advance. The ground was so shattered into shell holes that the men had some cover as they dropped into and crawled out of the massed craters. Bennett later said, 'we were like a swarm of rats in a ploughed field'. Under the advancing onslaught the Germans fled their trenches, which were taken by the Worcesters. The small surviving force continued their attack along the whole length of the trenches and dug into a new line beyond the captured ground. Although under constant counterattack, they held firm all day until being relieved at nightfall, by which time Bennett could only muster about sixty men, out of the original 300 or so, with whom to fall back behind the lines. The battalion diary's usual understatement describes him as having 'led the battalion and [done] conspicuous good work'. The line they consolidated was named Bennett Trench in his honour. His bravery and fine leadership was rewarded with the Victoria Cross.

His citation in the *London Gazette* on 30 December 1916 read:

> For most conspicuous bravery in action when in command of the second wave of the attack. Finding that the first wave had suffered heavy casualties, its commander killed and the line wavering, Lt. Bennett advanced at the head of the second wave, and by his personal example of valour and resolution reached his objective with but sixty men.
>
> Isolated with his small party, he at once took steps to consolidate his position under heavy rifle and machine gun fire from both flanks, and although wounded, he remained in command, directing and controlling.
>
> He set an example of cheerfulness and resolution beyond all praise, and there is little doubt that but for his personal example of courage, the attack would have been checked at the outset.

The *Stroud News* that week concluded its editorial with its usual patriotic enthusiasm: 'It is such acts as this that stamp the seal of superiority of British Troops. Led by such officers the men will go anywhere, and all the ingenious human-killing machinery invented by the Germans cannot stop them.'

Lieutenant Bennett spent several months back in England recovering from his wounds and it was not until February 1917 that he was able to attend Buckingham Palace again to receive his VC from the King. He returned to Stroud on 21 February 1917, where he was greeted at the station by the Town Council, a guard of honour and his family. Huge crowds lined the streets to welcome him home and a celebratory dinner in his honour was given at the Holloway Institute.

In October 1918 he had recovered sufficiently from his wounds to return to France as a captain with the 4th Battalion Worcestershire Regiment, in time to join them at the Battle of Courtrai in Belgium. However, just four days later, on 14 October (and just four weeks before the Armistice), he was severely wounded by an exploding shell fragment and was again evacuated to England, where he was laid up in bed with multiple wounds for almost a year, after which he returned to civilian life.

The Bennetts were one of the Stroud district's more active and involved families. Parents Charles and Florence lived in the 1880s and '90s at Derry Hay, now Victory Park, Cainscross, where their six children were born and father Charles was headmaster at Cainscross Elementary School.

By 1901 they had moved home to Fromehurst (now Longcroft) in Frome Park Road, Rodborough where Paul and his younger brother Theodore attended Rodborough School. The family was very busy around the parish and town; Charles had become chief secretary of the Stroud Conservative Workingmen's Benefit Society as well as Rodborough church organist, choirmaster, Bible class leader and Sunday school superintendent. He was involved in organising most local music concerts at which he, his wife, daughter and five sons would all take part, playing instruments, singing or recitation. Sporty sons Harold, Paul and Theodore also played rugby and cricket for the parish and the town.

Talented though they were, it was a family which experienced more than its fair share of tragedy, losing four of its menfolk between 1914 and 1919. Leopold died of pneumonia in 1914, aged 23. Harold, a Royal Garrison Artillery Second Lieutenant, died in 1915 in a motorcycle accident in Cardiff, aged 25. Then, after serving throughout the war in France and Egypt, the youngest of the boys, Lieutenant Theodore Bennett, was killed in action aged 24 in Palestine with the 1st/5th Worcesters on 7 September 1918. Only a year later, in September

Theodore and Paul Bennett at Rodborough School, c. 1904. (Courtesy of Jonathan Briggs)

1919, their father Charles also died following a hospital operation in London. Paul was still in hospital recovering from the terrible wounds he received the previous year in Belgium and was unable to attend his father's funeral.

Paul had been born on 4 June 1892 and in 1919 he was just 27 years old, having matriculated from Marling School, worked for the Bank of England in London, spent four years in France during the Great War witnessing death around him almost daily, displayed enough courage in action to win both a Military Cross and a Victoria Cross, been severely wounded twice and seen three brothers die, as well as his father. Enough incident and experience for a lifetime perhaps, but he had only just started. After the war and his recovery he moved back to London and married songwriter Violet Forster at Kingston, Surrey, in July 1922. They had a daughter, Elizabeth (known as Toodles) in 1923, and a son, Jonathan, in 1931, who sadly died of pneumonia in 1946 while at Eton.

In 1923 Paul became a lawyer, was called to the Bar at Middle Temple, London, and served as Prosecuting Council on the South East Circuit between 1931 and 1935. Subsequently he was a Metropolitan Magistrate until 1961. He was also a Governor of the Regency Polytechnic College. During the Second World War his family home was in Marylebone, London, which was bombed on two occasions. During that period he was a squadron leader in the Air Training Corps of the RAF. In the later years of his life he retired to Vicenza, near Venice in Italy with his wife Violet, and died there on 6 April 1970 aged 77. A remarkably full life by any standards.

3
RODBOROUGH

JULIE MOUNTAIN

In the early twentieth century, the large and scattered parish of Rodborough was formed by the settlements of Rodborough, Kingscourt and Butterrow, each with a school and a church or chapel. From the River Frome on the east, the boundary veered west, encompassing Swellshill, Houndscroft and Little Britain Farm, and running down into the Nailsworth Valley. Lightpill and Dudbridge housed industry and provided employment for many of the parishioners. The border of Rodborough with Stroud was marked by the river at Wallbridge.

In 1914 the parish council gave the population as 3,721 in 998 households. Rodborough was well-served; Kelly's Directory of 1914 lists eleven shopkeepers, a butcher, two bakers, two dairymen, a greengrocer, The Bear Hotel, six pubs and eleven beer retailers. Post offices were situated at The Butts, Bath Road, Butterrow and Lightpill, with a police station at Lightpill.

The rector of the parish church, Revd Walter Waring, had been in post since 1897 and continued to officiate throughout the war years. He had baptised some of the boys and married many of the young men who went off to war; a few of whose battered bodies he later interred in the churchyard. In 1915 he was responsible for compiling a roll of Rodborough men who had enlisted, published in May in the *Stroud News*. Such lists were a means of encouraging recruitment and Rodborough's list at that time contained 128 names.

In the early months of the war over fifty employees of the Dudbridge Ironworks Co. joined 'Lord Kitchener's Army' in one week. The ever patriotic *Stroud News* commented, 'Britain's manhood is now rousing itself from its lethargy and is about to put forth all its strength against the modern Huns who are devastating Europe'.

Rodborough Post Office at The Butts in the early twentieth century. (Courtesy of Howard Beard)

Meanwhile, the Butterrow Women's Bible Class was sending chocolates to the Glosters at the front, the lady in Rodborough post office was donating sweets and books for the wounded soldiers at the hospital, and Mrs Sims was giving clothes for Belgian refugees. The church reported a paucity of decoration at the Harvest Festival and a quieter Christmas.

Rodborough School's gardening class were doing war work cultivation at the weekend, so were able to send fruit and vegetables to the Royal Navy. The children were sending gifts to wounded soldiers and mittens to the front. The school logbook recorded a falling roll of children as many families of enlisted men had returned to the wife's former home. The usual hardships of the times continued; illness was rife and 1915 was a particularly bad year: in June the school was closed following an outbreak of German measles from which one little boy died. Early 1917 was one of the coldest winters on record: Rodborough School's toilets were almost continually frozen and it was a struggle to get the classroom temperature to just above 40°F (about 6°C).

At Kingscourt School in the 1914 Christmas concert Louis Marks sang 'My Soldier Daddy' – a song about a young child reassuring his mother that their prayers would be answered and Daddy would return from the war safe and well. What they weren't to know was that the tears and anguish of the war had barely begun.

Much later, in 1917, Mr John May, the headmaster of Kingscourt School, recorded in the logbook the pleasure of welcoming back Frank Davis, a recently injured ex-pupil who came in to talk to the children. Lance-Sergeant Davis of 2/5th Gloucesters had been awarded the Distinguished Conduct Medal and the French Medaille Militaire. (In 1920, along with other ex-scholars, Frank was a pall bearer at John May's funeral.) In later years Frank was remembered as a man who commanded local respect. His house in Kingscourt Lane is still called 'Vermand' today, after the town in northern France.

From the beginning of 1916 the Military Service Act brought conscription into effect. Men aged between 19 and 41, who were unmarried or widowed without dependent children, were expected to enlist, though anyone doing essential work was exempted. By May 1916 the Act had been extended to cover married men. Nationally over a million men appealed against conscription and local tribunals heard cases from individuals and employers on the grounds of ill health, serious hardship, conscientious objection, or that their employment was considered essential.

The Military Representative for Stroud Rural District Council was Lieutenant Wood. In July 1916 he reported that the Chief of Staff had declared that at least another million men would be required that year and the authorities were seriously concerned about the number of men that were being exempted, so though he was not anxious to send men to the front, he felt it was his duty to do so. Consequently, most appeals were, at best, successful in gaining only a month or two's grace. Over a prolonged period until the war ended, local firms were lodging appeals to try and hold on to their staff.

Numerous tribunal reports throughout the war show how difficult staffing was for local firms. Strachan's woollen manufacturers applied for the exemption of three men who were claimed to be crucial to the carrying on of the business at Fromehall Mills, half of the work being the manufacture of Naval cloth. The enlistments were merely deferred.

Messrs Apperly, Curtis & Co. Ltd of Dudbridge Cloth Mills applied for the exemption of the sole representative of the firm in the north-west of England. He was 36 years of age and lived in Southport. Lieutenant Wood said that travellers were luxuries now and the application was dismissed.

A little more success came in an application in June 1916 by Messrs Kimmins, Drew and Co. Ltd of Dudbridge on behalf of three carters. Mr Kimmins explained that he would not be appealing to retain workers inside the mill, but carters were difficult to replace, though he had advertised and applied at the Labour Exchanges, without luck, to try and secure men ineligible for military service. The youngest man, at 25 years of age, received a short exemption, the others were given several months.

During an appeal, Mr J.E. Mann, manager at Copeland-Chatterton account book manufacturers of Dudbridge, said the firm had lost twenty-two out of thirty-six eligible men with two more pending.

For small firms, the self-employed and those with dependants, the obligation to enlist caused great stress. A Wallbridge butcher, probably Walter Turner, listed in the 1914 Kelly's Directory, said he had no help and was the only butcher in the parish. Edward Beavis, a Rodborough builder, urged the exemption of a painter and paper-hanger, but the application was refused on the grounds that paper-hanging was not essential.

John Sandling, a 39-year-old Dudbridge basket maker, appealed on the grounds of hardship. He said his widowed father was an invalid and his only brother was serving with the 5th Gloucesters. His case was deferred but he eventually enlisted, returning to the family business after the war. John Sandling senior died in January 1917.

Lady Apperly of Rodborough Court also felt herself to be in straitened circumstances. She appealed in June 1916 to retain her gardener on the grounds that he was the only man on the estate. 'He would be 41 years of age in October and it was impossible to carry on a large and valuable property without him.' Exemption, for one month, was allowed. Lady Apperly had been widowed in 1913 and one of her sons, Arthur, had voluntarily enlisted in November 1915 and subsequently died at the Somme in August 1916.

Sandlings basket makers at Dudbridge. (Courtesy of Sue Francis)

Some of those in high-profile roles demonstrated their support through personal action. The chair of the parish council, former magistrate Frank Gwynne-Evans, though aged 43 and above the current criteria for conscription, enlisted in May 1916. In April 1918, a further extension of the Military Service Act raised the maximum age for enlistment to 50. Frederick Wake of Lightpill was a highly respected man who had begun his working life on the railways but had risen to become a magistrate and sat on the military tribunals' panel. Aged 44 and prevented from enlistment only by virtue of his occupation, he tendered his resignation, saying that the new regulations 'placed him in a very invidious position'. At the time this decision was made and as yet unknown to Frederick, his own son, also named Frederick, who had been serving in France, had just died, aged 19, as a prisoner of war in Germany.

For one newly conscripted man the prospect was unbearable. Henry John Lusty, a brickworker of Meadow End, Dudbridge, was found dead at Woolwich Barracks in July 1916. His wife had said farewell to him at Dudbridge station and later commented that he appeared quite cheerful, but had only returned to work a fortnight before, having recently suffered from influenza. His body was found against a tree with a wound to his throat and knife held in his right hand. The inquest recorded a verdict of 'suicide during temporary insanity'. He is buried in a Commonwealth War Grave in Woolwich Old Cemetery but his name is not recorded on Rodborough's war memorial.

For others, however, enlisting was an attractive option. Two Rodborough boys are known to have enlisted well under age. One was Jack Stockwell of Bath Road, an employee of the *Stroud News*, who reported that his enthusiasm for war 'has been a bit of a worry to his employers and parents'. Jack joined the colours at a very early stage of the conflict and it was only when he was down for a draft that it was discovered he was under age. In August 1918 he legally joined the navy and the *Stroud News* wished him good luck 'despite the turmoil he caused in this office by his patriotic fervour'! The other Rodborough lad was Frederick Arthur Hawkins of 5 Field Road, who was only 14 when he enlisted. He served for 182 days in the UK before being rumbled and discharged!

Records of serving women are sparse. Miss Dorothy David of Lightpill joined the Motor Transport division of the Army Service Corps in 1917, having already relinquished school teaching for a position as a driver at the Stroud garage of Messrs H.E. Steel Ltd. Local newspaper reporting praised her 'pluck and enthusiasm and spirit of derring do'.

Estimates given at the end of the war number men serving from Rodborough at over 400. Largely unrecorded are the stories of those who went off to war and survived the experience. One such man was farmer Reg James of Stringers

Farm, who took two horses from the farm and joined the Yeomanry Brigade of the Royal Gloucestershire Hussars. He sustained a leg wound in Gallipoli in 1915 during the attack on Chocolate Hill, but, making a good recovery, he eventually re-joined his unit in Palestine where he was involved in the retirement from El Salt. He was a Hotchkiss machine gunner and was mentioned in despatches for his coolness under fire. By firing bursts from the continuous metallic strips of ammunition, his troop held off the Turks, who were moving in open formation through a field of corn. Later he took part in Lord Allenby's historic advance through Palestine as far north as Damascus; a campaign which saw the downfall of the Ottoman Empire which had dominated the Middle East for centuries. Reg's war story was recorded in the notes of a local journalist, but his family said he never spoke about his ordeal. There is no record of what became of the horses, but Mr James was awarded two medals which were donated to the Royal Glos Hussars Charitable Trust in Cirencester.

Serving with Reg was Trooper Harry Smith, a former postman of Rodborough, who sent letters about himself and 'Reggie' to Mr and Mrs Ellis of Rodborough post office. They were reported as taking a 'kindly interest in the soldiers from their parish' and further circulated the news in the 'With the Colours' column of the *Stroud News*. In one letter Harry thanks them for sending a photo of Rodborough church.

After the war Reg James returned to Stringers Farm and resumed farming, eventually taking over from his father and expanding the dairy business. He also served on the Commons Committee, as had his father and grandfather before him. He was often to be seen repairing fencing, rounding up stray cattle and maintaining water supplies. He died in 1972.

Mrs Amy Ellis was seemingly a regular correspondent to the *Stroud News*. In September 1917 she sent in a poem entitled 'Our V.C.' about Rodborough's Paul Bennett (mentioning also that Harry Smith had sung alongside Paul in Rodborough church choir):

On land and sea, brave deeds are done,
Hard fights are fought, big battles won,
Which makes us of our soldiers proud,
So welcome back, brave Paul of Stroud.

In this our own, dear native land,
We quietly rest, nor understand,
How Belgium's fields are as a shroud,
To hide her dead, brave Paul of Stroud.

Battles' sad sights, the cannons roar
Is sounding now, from shore to shore,
When peace shall come; with Prussians cowed
Come home to us, brave Paul of Stroud.

Brothers and sons, we hail you all.
Answering so nobly, your country's call.

Amy E. Ellis

In 1918 the local newspapers promoted an active fundraising campaign for St Dunstan's, a charity for blind former servicemen formed in 1915. Among many soldiers to lose their sight was James Pile, a painter and decorator of Prospect Cottage, Butterrow West. James was a 36-year-old father of three when he first went to France with the 5th Gloucesters in 1916. In 1917 he was severely wounded and shell shocked and as a consequence lost his sight and his memory. He was treated in Tooting Military hospital, where he was pictured in his 'hospital blues'. After the war he received training from St Dunstan's but his impaired memory restricted his employment.

James' youngest brother, Leonard Pile, was killed in France in 1917.

Meanwhile, in Rodborough, local firm T.H. & J. Daniels at Lightpill and the Dudbridge Ironworks had turned to the production of munitions. The Daniels family were local landowners and also utilised their staff on the land in the absence of farmworkers. The work was undoubtedly long and hard, but the employers took pains to organise social events such as the munitioneers' fêtes at Fromehall Park. The employment of women in industry helped to alleviate struggles with staffing, along with those men who could be retained, and some travelled by special trains from Stroud to the filling factory (Gloucester's National Filling Factory No. 5) at Quedgeley. Here shells and cartridges were filled with explosives. Pay was comparatively good, particularly as large numbers of the women employed are reported to have come from domestic service, but much of the work involved handling dangerous chemicals, including TNT, with little protection. Consequently, many of the workers developed toxic jaundice and were nicknamed 'canaries' due to the yellowing of their skin.

Julia Stockwell of Bath Road, Rodborough was a munitions worker who tragically fell victim to many of the ills of the era. Julia married her sweetheart Sgt Arthur Watkins on 27 October 1917. Following the wedding, Julia returned to her job at the filling factory in Quedgeley and Arthur to the Gloucestershire Regiment. He was killed in action on the Western Front five months later and

James Pile with his wife Louisa and children Walter (standing), Cissie and Billy at Prospect Cottage, Butterrow West. (Courtesy of Margaret Tyler)

T.H. & J. Daniels' machine shop workers, 1918. (Courtesy of the Museum in the Park, Stroud)

Julia died on the first anniversary of their wedding in 1918; one of the first victims of the flu epidemic which had claimed a significant numbers of lives in Stroud by October 1918. Her death certificate also lists pernicious anaemia as a secondary cause of death and it raises the question of whether the true diagnosis might have been jaundice due to chemical poisoning.

As the war years lingered, food economy began to bite. Amongst numerous regulations from the Ministry of Food was the 1917 Bread Order, prohibiting the sale of bread less than twelve hours old, in order to reduce consumption. The rationale was that freshly baked bread was difficult to slice thinly and so appetising that it was difficult to resist eating moderately. Frederick Hiron Poole, a baker of Butterrow, was one of many caught in breach of the order, when PC Clifford found 125 loaves of hot bread in his cart at Rodborough. In his defence Mr Poole said that due to the flu epidemic causing other bakers to be unable to function, demand was more than he could supply in stale bread. He was fined £5.

To help the community deal with rising prices Mr Owen Paddison of Bownham House and Mrs Edith Ingram of Robinswood, Frome Park Road, were instrumental in forming a Food Committee for Rodborough in May 1917. The committee gave advice about the preserving of food and supplied jars for bottling at low prices. Following on from this, Mr Paddison took an active role in the ambitious Patriotic Economy Exhibition held at Stroud Subscription Rooms in June, with Mrs Ingram closely involved. Rodborough Girl Guides formed a guard of honour to welcome Countess Bathurst, who opened the exhibition.

Rodborough appears to have been unique locally in owning a fruit evaporator. It is not clear whether the device was bought or made, but it was installed in the cookery room of Rodborough School in September 1917. Its function was the drying of fruit in order to preserve without the use of sugar. No photos of the apparatus exist, but it is described as a wooden cabinet containing trays with perforated metal bases. Gas burners in the base of the cabinet circulated heat. Each tray projected a few inches in front of the one above, so that the space at the back formed a hot air chamber and the heat passed through the trays of fruit to escape with the moisture at the front. The process required constant supervision from Mrs Ingram and her team of ladies. Local residents were invited to bring in prepared fruit; plums whole, apples cored and sliced into rings and pears quartered. Baskets were left with a self-addressed postcard which would be returned to notify when to collect the dried fruit and only cost around a penny per pound of fruit. It was hoped that later the process would be adapted to deal with potatoes and vegetables and the Rodborough Food Committee were prepared to lend out the fruit drier locally.

Rodborough Gardening Association's exhibition at Rodborough School, 8 October 1921. (Courtesy of Howard Beard)

Along with the Rodborough Gardening Association, an exhibition was held in October 1918 at Rodborough School displaying bottled fruits, jams, vegetables etc. The afternoon ended with an 'experimental war tea', offering cakes made without eggs and with sugar substitutes. Lady Apperly, opening the event, said she hoped it would become an annual event and this appears to have been so, as evidenced by Rodborough Gardening Association's exhibition at Rodborough School in 1921.

Many local residents contributed to the war effort. In 1918 Edward Cockett, a pigeon-flying enthusiast of Bath Road, was invited by the government to breed homing pigeons. Having lost a son to the war in 1916, he may have been more ready than most to help. The Army Pigeon Service employed around 3,000 men and the birds released from the trenches carried important messages in a small metal canister attached to the leg.

The women of Rodborough responded to a moving appeal published in the *Stroud News* in 1917, requesting readers to make hospital bags for soldiers. Specific directions were given for the construction of a small drawstring cloth bag with a white calico name label, intended to hold a soldier's personal belongings when he was admitted to hospital and to prevent their loss as he moved through the system. Bright coloured fabrics were suggested and a report from *The Times* was quoted, saying how much the little chintz bag or bag with roses had meant. One soldier said, 'it reminded me of the cushions and covers at home'. A mother said that the little bag bearing her dead son's name and address had enabled his belongings to be returned to her.

Although much of the quiet work and forbearance of vast numbers of women in Rodborough has passed unrecorded, a rather emotional tribute was paid to Mrs Lucy Waring, the vicar's wife, in December 1918 when she was presented with a silver teapot and album by the parishioners. In his address, Mr Browne, headmaster of Rodborough School, commended the work of all women at home, in hospitals and supply depots, and in uplifting the hearts of those who suffered due to the wounding and death of loved ones. Of Mrs Waring, he remarked that those present knew of her loving devotion to her suffering sisters. He had met her in all hours and in all weathers doing her splendid work. Moved by the occasion, Lucy Waring said she had loved the work and saw how brave their women were and how patiently they had borne their anxieties and sufferings.

On 4 August 1918, marking four long years of war, churches in Stroud and throughout the land held 'Remembrance Day' services. A large gathering took place at the Woodchester Wayside Cross. Thankfully the end was soon to come.

The reception of the ending of the war was recorded beautifully in the Kingscourt School logbook:

This morning soon after 11 o'clock the sound of hooters and church bells made us aware of the fact that the armistice between the Allies and Germany had been signed. The village was wild with excitement. The men were coming up from the mills having closed down for the day, and some were marching about ringing handbells. Work in school was out of the question so we had a short address on the meaning of the event interspersed with bell ringing outside, then the National Anthem followed by three cheers and sent the children home. During the dinner hour messengers from Stroud brought the news that it had been decided to close the schools for the day. The pending termination of the Great War is the source of intense gratification to the whole nation. [In red ink in the margin are the carefully written words 'ARMISTICE NOV 11th 1918'.] (Courtesy of Gloucestershire Archives, ref. S272/2/1)

Rejoicing continued the following day among the stalwarts of Rodborough's industry. A procession headed by a fife band and made up of men and women from Dudbridge Iron Works, T.H. & J. Daniels, Phoenix, Apperly's and other mills, made its way from the Dudbridge Iron Works to King Street Parade in Stroud, where an enthusiastic address was given by Mr John Daniels. He said that 'although the victory had been won by the soldiers and sailors, great credit was due to the vast army of factory workers, who in a quiet, unostentatious and devoted manner had done their duty nobly in the great national crisis'.

Peace celebrations were held throughout the nation on 19 July 1919. Rodborough had made the decision to defer the event until the August Bank Holiday; a good plan in retrospect as 19 July was a very wet day.

The celebrations were on an ambitious scale. A procession of motor cars, children in fancy dress and lorries to carry the little ones wended from the flagpole at the foot of the Fort. The route down Rodborough Hill and along the Bath Road to Fromehall Park was lined with flag-waving spectators at the roadside and in windows decorated with streamers. As the procession approached the Golden Cross the band played an emotive 'Where are the boys of the old brigade?' At the foot of one of the sloping gardens, a makeshift cenotaph had been erected, with a laurel wreath and the inscription 'our heroes beloved'. At this point, in the day of mixed emotions, an act of remembrance took place, though Revd Waring was attired in a top hat, dress suit and rosette.

Processing through the Lodge Gates of Fromehall Park, there followed ex-servicemen, schoolchildren, Scouts, Girl Guides, a bicycle section and a party of buglers. In a mix of religious and ceremonial, Charles Apperly spoke from his car and the throng sang 'All people that on earth do dwell' and the national anthem, before the festivities began.

There were sports, including a pillow fight, a ladies' nightdress and candle race, and a men's somersault and roll race! In a marquee a roast tea was beautifully presented to 1,000 children in three sittings, the logistics of which would challenge modern catering. An evening of music, dancing and fireworks followed.

The following day a 'Merry smoking concert' was held at the Subscription Rooms, providing dinner for 'over 800 servicemen and ex-servicemen' (as reported by the *Stroud News* – possibly an exaggeration of numbers). The waitresses wore Union Jack aprons. Eugene Paul Bennett, awarded the VC in 1916, sent a letter of apology saying he was in bed with a 'Blighty one'.

It is hard to be sure of the accuracy of estimates of men involved, but in trying to comprehend the scale of local involvement in Spillman's Road alone eight men gave their lives during the course of the war and from the Bath Road, between Wallbridge and Lightpill, fifteen men were lost.

The question of Rodborough having a war memorial was first raised by Mr Wake in March 1919 at a rather stormy parish meeting. It was reported that the parish council had already made an application for a German gun, 'as a war trophy'. It was suggested it could be displayed in a prominent place with the names of the war dead affixed. Lively debate followed. The chairman dryly suggested they should 'bury the gun'! On the subject of something more useful,

Crowds at The Golden Cross on Peace Day, 1919. (Courtesy of Howard Beard)

Mr Payne suggested the need of a drinking fountain on the Common. The parish church vestry committee suggested a lychgate, choir stalls or new motor for the organ! Over the following months further discussions ensued with much difference of opinion.

In June there was a large parish meeting. The general consensus was that a memorial hall for Rodborough would fit the bill. Interestingly the dissenting parties were Mr Wake and Mr Cockett, both of whom had lost sons. They favoured a column of plinth panels depicting the horrors of war. Mr Wake conceded that this could be combined with a memorial hall. Mr Cockett's desire was to end all wars and this could only be done by impressing on children the horrors of war and he did not think a hall would do that.

By the end of 1920 most villages locally had a memorial in place. Rodborough was fundraising throughout the year for the memorial hall. The last reported fundraising event was a garden fête held in the Rectory Gardens on 17 July, by which time £2,200 of the required £4,000 had been raised and Mr Beavis, the builder, had offered a piece of land. For reasons that are not clear, however, Rodborough never did have the proposed war memorial hall.

The church vestry minutes show that the current memorial was discussed and planned in July 1920 in a very business-like manner. The only matter of contention was that the diocese insisted the words 'To the glory of God' be removed from the original design. Fundraising began for the £62 required. A house-to-house collection was organised and 'The Chairman pointed out to each collector that every care should be taken to make it clearly understood that this fund is in no way connected with the Rodborough Parish Memorial Institute Fund'.

The war memorial tablet unveiled in November 1921 is located on the north wall inside St Mary Magdalene church, off Walkley Hill. It now bears sixty names, initially listed alphabetically; five names were added to the base at a later date. The memorial was created for the parish from Painswick stone by local monumental masons Freebury and Hillman Ltd, who made many others in the area and also contributed masonry for the Menin Gate Memorial to the missing in Belgium. The cost of £62 was raised by public subscription. The small remaining funds were used to purchase a wooden font cover with a commemorative brass plaque, still in use today.

Arguably there are a number of war dead who deserved a place on the war memorial and it is unclear why their names were omitted. One such is Charles Burroughs, who lies buried with his brother, Frank, in Rodborough churchyard beneath a simple iron cross, thought to be made by their father Richard, an iron moulder.

Charles, the middle of seven children, lived in the steep narrow lane of Court Bank, off Butterrow Hill. Only one property remains today, but the 1911 census records fifty-one people in nine houses there. Charles signed up for the Gloucestershire Regiment on 19 August 1914, just before his 20th birthday. A slight figure at 5ft 2in tall, weighing 7st 9lbs and with a fully expanded chest of 34 inches, he gave his occupation as a cook. In July 1916, serving with the 8th Gloucesters at High Wood, he sustained dreadful abdominal injuries while taking part in the Somme offensive. Subsequently contracting tuberculosis, Charles returned home and was discharged as medically unfit for war service. After three years of illness and spending time at Cranham Lodge Sanatorium, he died of tuberculosis at Over Hospital for Infectious Diseases on 26 March 1919, aged 24. His younger brother, Frank, died of the same condition in Stroud General Hospital just three months later.

Charles' death was not recognised by the Commonwealth War Graves Commission but as a result of recent research this has now been amended. His medals are housed at Stroud's Museum in the Park.

In 2013, research into the names recorded on the war memorial began. Some of the stories have unfolded easily, particularly where documents or artefacts exist. The extraordinary confirmation of the death of Arthur Harris, of Bath Road Terrace, was made by the touching gesture of a German soldier.

Arthur had been six weeks from completion of an ironfounder's apprenticeship at the works of T.H. & J. Daniels of Lightpill when, being a part-time Territorial, he was called up in August 1914. On 22 October 1917 the Gloucesters 14th (service) Battalion, with whom Arthur was then serving, saw action in the Houthulst Forest north of Ypres as part of the Third battle of Ypres, otherwise known as Passchendaele. He never returned and was listed 'missing in action'. Normally this would be the end of the story, but in 1918 a letter was received by the British authorities in England, via The Red Cross, from a German soldier in the trenches where Arthur had died. It stated that his body was lying in front of the German trench and enclosed was his identity disc as confirmation of his death 'in order to spare his relatives useless and painful doubts or hopes'. The original letter and tag are held at the Soldiers of Gloucestershire Museum.

Hamlyn Clifford Lane, known as Clifford, also lived in Bath Road Terrace. As a known prisoner-of-war in 1918, he was expected home after peace was declared. His sister Dorothy regularly met the incoming troop trains, to no avail, and his sad story is pieced together in a series of letters.

Clifford was born on 11 July 1899, the youngest child of Edward and Elizabeth Lane. Having attended Rodborough School and served as an apprentice pattern-maker at Stroud Metal Company in Dudbridge, he joined up in 1917. He had passed the entrance exam for the Royal Flying Corps, but as they had no vacancies he joined the Warwickshire Regiment, later transferring to the Royal Berkshires.

In a letter home in March 1918, Clifford said he was to be posted abroad the following day and he hoped that the current battles would bring peace before his regiment 'goes up the line'. On 27 May, barely two months later, Clifford was captured in Fisines, France and became a prisoner-of-war. A few weeks later the anxious family received news that he was missing in action.

He sent four postcards home, one of which was a picture postcard stating, 'I am quite well, although a Prisoner of War, but don't worry, I will write as soon as possible'.

In an undated letter he says he is well, but not strong, asks for his mates to be told of his plight, recounts the feast he had in the trenches from a parcel the family had sent in May, and asks if they can send him an exercise book and some envelopes, a razor, comb, mirror and any foodstuff, 'though I don't want to rob Les [his brother in France] of a parcel'.

Nothing further was heard from Clifford, but the family felt no cause for worry and confidently expected his arrival home. It was not until December 1918 that the family was informed by the Red Cross of his death. The formal Infantry Record Office letter did not arrive until January 1919; it announced that Clifford had died on 23 July, just weeks after his last communication. His personal effects were finally returned to the family on 27 April 1920 and in 1924 the Imperial War Graves Commission wrote to say that he had been

Children at Rodborough School, c. 1904. Clifford Lane is second from the right in the second row. Alongside him are his brothers Leslie left, Stanley right and sister Dorothy (fourth from the right). The photo also shows Paul Bennett (third from the right in the third row) who was awarded the VC, alongside his brother Theo (fourth right), who was killed. On the far left on the front row is Jack Stockwell, who enlisted underage. Standing above him is Ed Cockett, who died at the Somme. (Courtesy of Jonathan Briggs)

Clifford Lane whilst training at Cramlington, Northumberland. (Courtesy of Jonathan Briggs)

exhumed from his original grave and re-interred at Sissonne British Cemetery, 'in order to secure the reverent maintenance of the grave in perpetuity'.

One of the most poignant mementos is a letter beginning 'My Dear Daddy' sent from the young son of Arthur Sydney Wright and kept safe by the family for over 100 years.

Arthur was born in 1883 in Hartpury near Gloucester, but his father died months later, leaving a widow to bring up six children alone. By 1914, Arthur's own family life seemed good. He was married to Estelle and living in a new house in Elm Terrace, Lightpill (now 28 Kitesnest Lane) with three small sons, the youngest born in August 1914. Arthur left his job as a compositor with Copeland-Chatterton Co. at Dudbridge to volunteer for service in 1914. His medal card indicates that he entered France on 3 November 1915.

Arthur was wounded at Back Wood on the Somme by heavy shell fire and he died of his wounds the following day, 23 August 1916. After his death, Estelle, who had never been physically strong, moved back to Gloucester to be close to her father, the monumental stonemason F.J. Cambridge, whose business continues today. Tragically, Estelle died of tuberculosis at the end of 1919 and the three orphaned boys were sent to live with relatives in Twigworth, near Gloucester.

It is believed that three of the men listed on the memorial were from travelling families; here the facts have been harder to establish, due to the nature of their lives.

William Stevens and William Allen are both buried in Rodborough churchyard with Commonwealth War Graves Commission headstones. Both died in hospitals in Gloucestershire. The newspapers of the period carry many references to the extended Stevens family (documented as Stephens), linked to minor transgressions of the law.

William Stevens, son of William and Elizabeth, served from 1914 and died of horrific injuries after the war ended, aged around 23. His military record survives and indicates that he had dark brown hair, blue eyes and a fresh complexion. Further it tells that he suffered gunshot wounds to his left hand and fingers at the Battle of Loos in September 1915 with the 10th Gloucesters and was punished for being absent from parade in the trenches with five days' Field Punishment Number 1: a very unpleasant punishment of being tied to a wooden cross or cartwheel for hours on end in a prominent place and unable to move. Worse was to follow. On 24 September 1916 he was engaged in 'The hell of High Wood' on the Somme, where a severe gunshot wound to the back left him with a fractured spine, paralysed legs and incontinent. He was, of course, discharged as 'permanently unfit for military service' and died after two years of bed-ridden suffering in the Royal Infirmary at Gloucester.

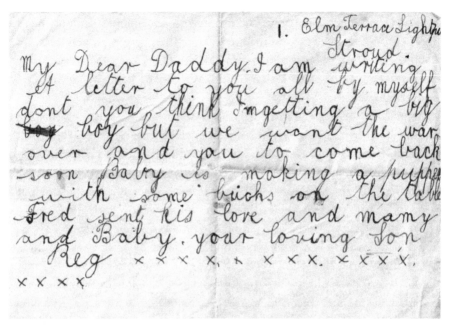

1. Elm Terrace Lightpill

Stroud.

My Dear Daddy. I am writing a letter to you all by myself dont you think Im getting a big boy but we want the war over and you to come back soon Baby is making a puppet with some bricks on the table. Fred sent his love and mamy and Baby. your loving son Reg x x x x, x x x x. x x x x. x x x x

Letter written by Arthur Sydney Wright's eldest son William Reginald Wright, aged about 7. (Courtesy of Pamela Brogan)

Fred, Arthur and Reg Wright, c. 1915. (Courtesy of Pamela Brogan)

It is of note that two of William Stevens' cousins, Andrew and William Leonard Stevens, sons of Leonard and Prudence, are recorded on the Nailsworth War Memorial, and William Leonard is also on the Woodchester Wayside Cross. We believe they are linked to the Stevens clan camped on Rodborough Common at the time of the 1881 census.

The Allen family appear to be connected to the Stevens' by marriage. Henry, a road labourer and licensed hawker, unable to sign his name, and Mazilla (or sometimes Priscilla) lost two sons. They are seen on various census records: in a shed at Rockness Hill, near Horsley, and a caravan on Selsley Hill. One of their children was born at Rubble Hole, the old name for the area below Little London, on the edge of Rodborough Common, and they have been recorded as living at Tabernacle Walk in Rodborough.

Corporal George Allen was the last Rodborough man to be killed in action on 20 October 1918, aged 19. George had been a farmworker and was a Lewis gunner with the 8th Gloucesters. His captain spoke highly of his conduct and said that having killed two Germans with his revolver, George was shot from behind by a German who had escaped the barrage and was hiding in a small trench. He described the exact spot near Cambrai where George was buried.

Of his brother, William Allen, we have more information. He was a small man with brown eyes and dark brown hair, a farm labourer noted to be of good character. He sustained gunshot wounds in 1914, though returned to France in 1915 and soon after was discharged as medically unfit. Dying aged 23 in 1917, his death certificate raises more questions than it answers. The cause of death was pulmonary tuberculosis, but occurred at Wotton Lawn Lunatic Asylum. It is mentioned in a newspaper report that he was 'badly gassed'. He was buried at Rodborough with full military honours.

Of the sixty plus Rodborough men who died, the first to die was Frederick Stockwell on 29 October 1914 and the last was Charles Burroughs on 26 March 1919. The youngest of Rodborough's war dead was Donald Brown, aged 17, and the oldest, at 48, was Alfred Street.

Officiating at the Peace Day in 1919 was Charles Bennett, who had lost two sons. To a hearty response, he said:

> The Rodborough boys had played a noble part in crushing the most terrible menace the world had ever seen. They had played a valiant part in the fight between right and wrong. He hoped God would enable them to carry into civil life the same virtues of courage, patience and forbearance which served them in such good stead when fighting the enemy.

4

A MINCHINHAMPTON PERSPECTIVE

DIANA WALL

THE CALL TO ARMS

In Minchinhampton, the early August Bank Holiday of 1914 was one of clear skies and warm sunshine, with residents enjoying the open spaces of the commons on this extra day off from work. Through the newspaper reports they would have read about the unfolding pattern of alliances in Europe since the assassination of Archduke Franz Ferdinand on 28 June, but it is unlikely that most saw this as relevant to their own lives. As people returned home in the late afternoon of Monday, 3 August the Foreign Secretary, Sir Edward Grey, outlined to Parliament the gravity of the situation and Britain's commitment to its allies on mainland Europe – most of the British public had no idea conflict was so close. An ultimatum to Germany demanding respect for Belgium's neutrality was given, but ignored; on 4 August Britain declared war. The following day the weather broke, and there was heavy rainfall in Gloucestershire.

> There has come upon us with startling suddenness the greatest war … which the world has ever seen … We are glad to know that so many from our parish have joined the King's Forces, but what of the rest of us? … If we think that duty calls us to fight for our country if need be, there is but one way to qualify ourselves – join Lord Kitchener's Army or the Territorials. (Revd F.D. Bateman, writing in Minchin Hampton [*sic*] Parish Magazine)

Several families from the town and villages around, like Amberley and Box, already had members serving in the regular armed forces. These were the first

Bank Holiday on Rodborough Common. (Courtesy of Minchinhampton Local History Group (MLHG) collection)

to feel the impact of the declaration of war. Henry and Constance Lawrence are recorded as purchasing Box House in 1893. In 1902 Henry died whilst at Box and of his four sons only Malcolm Eyton and Christopher Hal reached adulthood. Christopher was a member of the Officer Training Corps at Trinity College, Cambridge and applied for a commission on the day war was declared. Two weeks later he was made second lieutenant in the King's Royal Rifle Corps and sailed for France in September. His death came during the Battle of the Aisne, on 13 October 1914; the records show he was killed by a sniper.

Meanwhile, following his degree, Malcolm had left England for Canada in 1911. He too was a reservist and came over with the first contingent of the Canadian Expeditionary Force. Upon landing, he was told of his younger brother's death and he applied for a commission in the King's Royal Rifle Corps, which was granted. In early December he went to France and at the beginning of 1915 he gained promotion to lieutenant. However, on 10 January he was killed in action near Givenchy whilst leading a storming party. The deaths of the two brothers exemplify the loss of experienced officers in the first months of the war; most brigades suffered similar deaths.

At the other end of the social scale were two more brothers, Albert and William Townsend, whose family had a strong military tradition. Their father, William Henry Townsend, enlisted in the 4th Battalion Gloucestershire Regiment (a militia battalion) in 1886 at Cirencester; a few months later he married Annie Reed, whose own father had been in the army before joining the police. Tragedy struck when William Henry died in 1899 and Annie struggled to keep the family together on the small army pension; by 1901 the two youngest boys, Ernest and Percy, were living in Stroud Union Workhouse. Both older boys joined the Gloucestershire Regiment as soon as they reached the minimum age, and the pay sent home enabled the younger boys to return to Annie, first in Tetbury Street, then Box and finally Forget-Me-Not Cottage in West End.

Albert was recalled to the 1st Battalion Gloucestershire Regiment on 2 August 1914 and went to France with the British Expeditionary Force soon afterwards. He went through several engagements, including the retreat from Mons in September, the counterattack and the establishment of trenches along the Somme Valley. The battalion was greatly depleted until reinforcements arrived in November. It was reported that Albert was shot in the head near the town of Festubert on 21 December 1914. He has no known grave and is commemorated on the Le Touret Memorial. William was with the 2nd Battalion Gloucestershire Regiment in 1914 when it was recalled from China, landing at Le Havre in December. The *Stroud News* reported that:

> … he passed safely through several engagements but his feet were badly frostbitten. He was invalided home in April and remained in England until August. He was married on the 17th July to Miss Hodges, whose home is at Ledbury. Then, attached to the 10th Gloucesters, he proceeded to France on 2nd August and again took part in several engagements. … At Loos … Corporal Townsend had his sleeve skimmed by a bullet. He and seven comrades were all who were left of one platoon (32 men) …

On the afternoon of 13 October 1915 the 10th Battalion took part in an assault on German positions but were heavily outgunned and the advance was a failure, resulting in the loss of 150 men killed, wounded or missing. Corporal Townsend was among the latter, but it was later confirmed he 'fell a true soldier and a man'.

There were other reservists, who had served in earlier conflicts, who were recalled to duty. From West End, Herbert Lines was to be engaged in recruitment, Tom Stratford, gamekeeper at Gatcombe Park, had served in the Boer War and would train these recruits. His employer, Major Henry George Ricardo, although well over 50 in 1915, returned to the Royal Field Artillery to provide support to the regimental administration; his three brothers of a similar age also responded to their regiments. However, with patriotic fever at a high pitch, it was the enlisting of volunteers which occupied the thoughts of many Minchinhampton folk in 1914.

In August many individuals from the town had volunteered to fight but it was in September that the main recruiting drive of the Stroud area took place. The *Stroud Journal* of 18 September 1914 reported:

Between 8 and 9 o'clock on Thursday morning in last week a good part of the inhabitants of Minchinhampton assembled near the Crown Hotel to witness the departure of the new recruits. Much enthusiasm was displayed, and a great deal of gratuitous advice of a cheering nature was given to the eighteen young fellows as they prepared to depart. Two evenings before leaving they were drilled in the park by Colonel James of Minchinhampton. Much of the work in connection with them has fallen on Corporal Herbert Lines, of West End and late of the Hunts Volunteers. He has been their paymaster and correspondent, and has taken much interest in their general welfare. He is also Hon. Secretary of the National Reserve.

Before leaving they were instructed to call on Mr. G. Castledine, High Street, where each one was presented with a packet of tobacco and a pipe. These were presented by the generosity of Mr. Fitzarthur Playne, Rev. J. R. Maul and Mr. Trollope. Corporal Lines, having read the roll-call, to which all the men responded, Major Ricardo gave them a brief address. He reminded them that they were responding to the call of their King and Country in the hour of need. He exhorted them to cheerfulness and courage, and wished them, in the name of their fellow citizens, God-speed. They then left the town amidst great enthusiasm. Many people followed them out of the town, and some of the school children followed them all the way to Stroud. They were conveyed in two brakes, decorated with the Union Jack, and were accompanied by Corporal H. Lines, who delivered them at the Armoury, Stroud at ten o'clock. The Minchinhampton Brass Band led them out of the town, playing patriotic airs.

Of the eighteen young men, four were to die on the Western Front, and three others were severely wounded or contracted illness overseas.

At the outbreak of the Great War, Frederick and Mary ('Minnie') Ellins of Friday Street had five sons and four daughters living at home. Frederick, aged 20, was a worker in a local carpet factory, but volunteered almost as soon as war broke out, joining the Gloucestershire Regiment. He went to Horfield Barracks in Bristol for initial training and arrived in France on 19 September 1914. The 1st Battalion was part of the British Expeditionary Force and had retreated from Mons before Frederick and the other volunteers arrived to boost numbers. The Gloucestershire Regiment then fought in what became known as the First Battle of Ypres. It was during this, on 7 November 1914, that Frederick was killed, but as his body was not recovered he is commemorated on the Menin Gate at Ypres.

Recruits outside the Crown Hotel, September 1914. From left to right are William Hatherall, Harry Young, Harry Wall, Charles Evans, George Cribley, Tom Stratford, Harold Young, -?- , Cyril Young, Ben Sparks, George Jukes (almost obscured), John Ellins, William Sessions, George Castledine, Arthur Breadmore, Lionel Day, William Butler, Harold Ponting, Ernie Harris, Frank Newman, Ernest Cook, Herbert Lines. (MLHG collection. The names were mainly provided by George Cribley in the 1980s, but with some additions based on research by families)

John, a year younger, leaving his job in a pin-making enterprise, is pictured holding a cornet in the centre of the picture of the recruits of September 1914. He, like most of those pictured, joined the 8th Battalion, Gloucestershire Regiment; their soldier numbers are sequential. This was part of Kitchener's New Army and joined the 1st and 2nd Battalions on the Western Front; the records show that John arrived in France on 18 July 1915. By 1916 he was in action in the Somme Offensive. The following year the battalion had moved into Flanders and entered the three-month long Third Battle of Ypres, or Passchendaele. Finally, in 1918, John was awarded the Military Medal for gallantry in the field, in the final push through northern France. John was one of the fortunate men who returned to Minchinhampton after the Armistice, honoured as one of the 'Comrades of the Great War'.

George tried many times to enlist by lying about his age. He was working in one of the local mills, manufacturing walking sticks and umbrella frames, but in 1916 was finally accepted into the Yorkshire and Lancashire Regiment. That same year his brother Matthew died, aged just 15. Following training, George was sent to France to fight in the trenches; in 1917 he received injuries to his face and back, but after a spell in England regaining his health he returned to the Western Front. His war record shows that he was wounded again, this time in his left leg, and was taken prisoner. He never complained about this but also never forgave the German 'rotter' who stole his last packet of Woodbines whilst he was in No Man's Land! In Stendal prisoner-of-war camp it was discovered that his wound had turned gangrenous and he received the news that his leg would have to be amputated, after his strength had been built up by living for a few days on an enhanced diet of eggs and meat. A report dated 27 September 1918 states that the Netherlands Legation had visited him, and that news of his amputation should be passed to his next of kin. He was no longer suitable for active service, so was repatriated in an exchange of prisoners set up by the Red Cross. His journey back to Minchinhampton was eventful too – he managed to sell his kit, and swapped his rail pass to Liverpool for one to Bristol! Youngest brother Albert was only 14 at the signing of the Armistice in 1918.

The Ellins brothers were employed in the mills of the valleys around Minchinhampton, but many others worked in agriculture – as labourers, carters, woodmen and gamekeepers. Their enlistment left serious labour shortages on local farms, with a resultant drop in food production. Harold and Cyril Young, aged 24 and 21, lived at Barcelona Farm and their cousin, Harry, also 24, was at Windmill Lodge. Both Harry and Cyril died in the first month of the Somme Offensive of 1916; they have no known grave and are commemorated with many other members of the Gloucestershire Regiment, including a further six from Minchinhampton, on the Thiepval Memorial.

STRETCHING INTO YEARS

'It must be a long time, probably as far back as the Civil War, since one who died of wounds in battle was buried in our churchyard'. (*Parish Magazine*)

On 15 September 1914, fighting near the River Aisne in northern France, Arthur Workman of 1st Battalion, Gloucestershire Regiment, was wounded in the forearm. Born in Minchinhampton, he was the son of Frederick and Hannah, who kept the King's Head public house at the Point in Forwood. However, he went to work as a machinist in local mills, and by 1911 was living with his elder brother, Frederick, in Swindon where his skills were employed at the Great Western Railway works. Later that year he returned to marry Mary Clark at Holy Trinity church, but they made their home in Swindon. Volunteering in 1914 he went to France with the British Expeditionary Force. Repatriated on medical grounds he went first to Plymouth, then, still suffering great pain, to Woolwich. Here it was found that the bullet had penetrated an artery, following a two-hour operation he died of heart failure. Private Workman's body was brought back to Minchinhampton and he was laid to rest with full military honours in Holy Trinity churchyard; his is one of four Commonwealth War Graves Commission (CWGC) graves from the Great War in that place.

When it became apparent that the war would not be over by Christmas, and that casualties were mounting, a system of casualty clearing stations were set up on the Western Front. From here the wounded were repatriated but the existing military hospitals, like that at Woolwich where Arthur Workman had died, were soon overwhelmed and a network of Red Cross Voluntary Hospitals was set up. The original plan was to develop a hospital in Minchinhampton at The Coigne in Market Square but when this idea was dropped it became the duty of the local Red Cross Committee to provide nurses, orderlies and cooks for the Nailsworth Hospital. This was established on 20 March 1915, at Chestnut Hill, the private home of Mr Clissold, who loaned it to the Red Cross for use as a 'Class B' convalescent hospital. Patients were transferred there mainly from Cirencester and Stroud VA hospitals.

A supply depot was set up in Minchinhampton, at The Gables, where donations of fruit, vegetables, cakes, jam as well as cigarettes or tobacco for the wounded were collected every week for Nailsworth. Longfords House became a War Hospital Supply Depot in October 1915, where groups of ladies met on Tuesdays and Thursdays to make bandages, swabs, dressings and pillows for

The staff and patients at Chestnut Hill House in 1915. The Commandant, Mrs Wilson, is seated centre. Behind her is Dr Bletchley and the three nurses to his left are from Minchinhampton. (MLHG collection)

hospitals and casualty clearing stations; again money was raised locally to buy the specialised materials necessary for this work.

Casualties continued to mount throughout 1915, both of local officers and those in the Pals' Battalions. By early 1916 the government saw no alternative but to increase numbers by conscription. In March 1916 the Military Service Act was passed which imposed compulsory active service on all single men aged between 18 and 41, but exempted the medically unfit, clergymen, teachers and certain classes of industrial worker. Conscientious objectors, who refused to fighting on moral grounds, were also exempted, and were in most cases given civilian jobs or non-fighting roles at the front; no record has been found of any conscientious objectors in Minchinhampton.

A second Act passed in May 1916 extended conscription to married men and those who enlisted after this date would be assigned by the recruiting office to any regiment which had suffered particular losses. Percy Townsend was one of the conscripts – his brothers, mentioned earlier, had both been killed – he was the third brother from West End to lose his life. There is no record of the fourth brother, Ernest, joining the colours, although he may have been medically unfit, as he died at an early age. In *Far From His Native Land He Lies*, Nick Thornicroft states:

> The stark realities of the deaths of the three Townsend brothers are these: all were killed in action during a major engagement which achieved little in the advancement of the Allies' fortunes and none was afforded a marked grave. The bereavement and catastrophic loss suffered by their mother, Annie, is impossible for us to comprehend.

One of the married men conscripted was Alfred Frederick Gabb, born locally in 1880 and baptised at Rodborough on 2 May of that year. He was the fifth child of Alfred Gabb and his wife Emma and a trade directory of 1879 describes Alfred Snr as a publican and butcher, the landlord of the Anchor Inn, Wallbridge. The family bought the butcher's shop in West End, Minchinhampton in 1903 and sold this in 1913 to a Frederick Buckland. In the 1911 census Alfred Frederick is shown as married to Amelia Rose from Maidenhead and living at West End, Minchinhampton, a few doors away from the police station; he is described as a journeyman butcher, aged 31 with four children.

Alfred was conscripted into the 8th Battalion, Gloucestershire Regiment when he was 36 years old. He only served a few months before he was killed in action in France on 28 July 1917; with no known grave he is commemorated on the Menin Gate at Ypres. Amelia Gabb did not remarry after her husband's death but continued to live in West End for some years, dying in Maidenhead in 1961.

In 1911 West End contained just over fifty dwellings; of these twelve were single-occupant almshouses. In the years of the Great War six young men from the street died, mirroring the scale of the sacrifices elsewhere in the parish.

THE HOME FRONT

During the Great War, 23,000 women were recruited nationally to work full-time on the land, to help replace men who had left to fight in the services and to increase home food production. The majority who worked in agriculture were milkers and field workers, but some were carters and plough-women working with horses as well as market gardeners. Lottie Bond (*née* Unwin) was living with her husband Albert and family at Besbury at the outbreak of war. Her husband had suffered ill health for some time, and, at the age of 47, she was undertaking work as a carter to support the family. Her eldest son, Albert Thomas, volunteered for the Gloucestershire Regiment in August 1914, her second son Hubert was 18 when conscription was introduced and probably served. Although her youngest son Charles was still a scholar, Lottie might have seen advertisements suggesting women working would enable more men to fight as she joined the Women's Land Army upon its formation in 1917. In addition to her haulage business, she worked in agriculture in this area, helping with all tasks on the farm; Lottie also worked for thirteen weeks in 1918 on the construction of Minchinhampton Aerodrome.

Upon moving to Besbury in 1913 sisters Gladys and Winnie Fitch soon became assimilated into the local community, making friends with others of the same age in the Playne and Beale families. From 1914 many of the young men they knew were fighting overseas, and it was this that spurred them on to undertake war work. Gladys, Winnie, Noel Playne and other Minchinhampton women all volunteered to work making munitions at the Phoenix Iron Works in Thrupp. Many of the foundries of the Stroud area produced brass shell cases that were sent by rail to Quedgeley to be filled with explosives. The female workforce, who were well paid by the standards then prevailing, all wore identical khaki clothing, with their heads covered – a far cry from the usual garb of the Fitch sisters to judge by their photograph albums. They worked long days – twelve-hour shifts were the norm – but were quick to learn the skills of drills, lathes and other heavy machinery.

The Kirby family, who lived in Church Cottage (now Vestry Cottage), exemplified the life of many families in Minchinhampton during the four years of the Great War. Much later, the oldest girl, Eva, remembered:

Lottie Bond in her Land Army uniform.
(Courtesy of the Bond family)

Winnie Fitch working on a lathe. (Courtesy of the Fitch family)

They had recruitment sessions in all the villages. Colonel Ricardo organised one and he stood on a platform in the Market Square asking for volunteers. My brother got up and volunteered, but my father stood up and said 'You can't have him! He's only seventeen.' But Archie went into Stroud the next day and joined up … Whenever he came home on leave, we were told not to ask him when he was going back. He'd come home in the middle of the night, after walking up from Stroud station. I can still remember how upset my mother was every time he had to go back … my grandfather would come to our house during the war with the daily paper and he used to sit down in our kitchen and say to my mother, 'Now I'll read 'ee the casualty list.' And he used to go all through the casualty list and my mother held her breath because, of course, my eldest brother was in the war. She was quite alright after grandfather got beyond the 'K's and she used to know her son was alright.

Eva's father was the Sexton at Holy Trinity church, and his life also took a busier turn. In 1916 the hours of evening services were brought forward (before double daylight saving was introduced) to comply with regulations on lighting, and one of his duties was to see that the congregation sat at the front of the nave, so there was no need for gas lighting in the aisles. The diocese recommended that insurance to cover damage from aircraft should be provided – special collections were made to defray the cost. He also ensured that not only his younger children, but those of his friends and neighbours, continued to attend school and Sunday school regularly. Here they used to pick blackberries, which were sent away to a factory to make blackberry jam for the troops, being paid a penny a pound for picking them. Eva remembered:

> There were many things to raise money for a Patriotic Fund. Every week a committee of ladies and helpers would go to the men's club – it used to be called the gymnasium – and they would cut out shirts and knit socks and balaclava helmets. My mother made a shirt most weeks all the years that the war was on.

Archie was one of the lucky ones who returned to Minchinhampton in 1919.

The effects of the continuing near-stalemate on the Western Front, coupled with shell-shock and physical wounds, led to tragic consequences for some civilians. In January 1915 Nellie Whiting of Hampton Fields, a 25-year-old girl working as a maid in Gloucester, was murdered by her sweetheart, William Fryer, a private in the 5th Battalion Gloucestershire Regiment. In January 1915 he had spent a week in Gloucester Gaol for insubordination; upon release he

Outside Church Cottage. Back row, from left to right, are John, Eva and Archie. Front: Bob, Mary, Sarah, Matt, Victor and Jessie. (MLHG collection)

was escorted to his parents' home where Nellie visited him. Barricading the door to his room, it appeared that he strangled her. At the trial he was found 'guilty but insane,' and following bouts of illness, died in Broadmoor Hospital in 1918.

A double tragedy took place on Sunday, 27 August 1916. Dorothy Beard, of Gravel Hill, Burleigh left home at 10.30 in the morning to meet her fiancé, Archibald Knee, at his home in West End. Archibald had been a cloth worker before being conscripted on 14 June 1916. He was a Private with 15th Battalion, Gloucestershire Regiment, aged 25, but had been home for a week on sick leave; during that time he told his family that he would rather die than go back. His father did his best to cheer him up and was under the impression that he would return to camp on Sunday; a car had been ordered to take Knee to the Great Western Railway station as he was due to return to Chiseldon. When Dorothy, a cloth weaver at Messrs P.C. Evans & Sons Ltd, Brimscombe, came to the house she, too, seemed somewhat depressed, probably at Archibald having to go back.

The couple left during the afternoon, Archibald to escort Dorothy home, but they failed to arrive. The Minchinhampton policeman, PC Dance, was alerted and their disappearance reported. The two fathers sat up all night and the next morning they made a search on the Common in the pools and reservoirs but without result. Their disappearance remained a mystery until Friday 1 September, when, just after noon, their bodies were discovered in Iron Mills Pond. They were tied together, face to face, with the man's raincoat, the knot which was behind the girl being made with the tails of his coat. They were both fully dressed and the military pass and railway ticket were found on Knee, as well as a purse containing 11 shillings. On the girl was a wristwatch which had stopped at 11 minutes to 4, a gold bangle, necklet and brooch.

According to the report of the inquest in the *Stroud News* published the following week:

> The jury returned a verdict in each case to the effect that they committed suicide by drowning themselves, there being no evidence to show the state of their minds. The Coroner, (Mr Morton Ball) said he was sure all wish to express sympathy with the families in their very grievous and terrible losses, and the jury agreed with these sentiments.

Dorothy Beard was buried at Amberley churchyard and Archibald Knee was interred at Minchinhampton Baptist graveyard. According to the *Stroud News*,

There was a large attendance of sorrowing relatives and friends at both interments. At Pte. Knee's funeral the Rev. S.J. Ford (pastor) officiated. Deceased had been a member of the Baptist Sunday School and before his death had attended the Sunday evening service at the Baptist Chapel, at which the Pastor made special reference to the young soldier who was about to return (as was then thought) to his military duties.

Indeed, a double tragedy for Minchinhampton, and also for the chapel, where Nellie Whiting had also been interred.

ARMISTICE, VICTORY AND COMMEMORATION

The signing of the Armistice occurred at 5.10 a.m. on 11 November 1918, at Compiegne in France. However, the actual ceasefire did not start until 11 a.m. to allow the information to travel to all parts of the Western Front. The news reached London by 5.40 a.m. and celebrations began before many soldiers knew about the Armistice; Big Ben was rung for the first time since the start of the war four years previously. Eva Kirby gives a personal account of that momentous day:

> One of the things I remember most about the end of the war was that the Armistice was signed on a Monday. My mother was doing the washing and she was so excited and so thrilled to think that the war was over, that during her washing she starched the woollen socks. I shall never forget the service we held in church on Armistice Day. The church was simply packed. Every time we hear now the hymn 'Now thank we all our God' I shall never forget that service. The people were crying and singing. It was the most wonderful day, when the war ended in 1918.

George Ludlow was working his market garden in Hampton Fields when the Armistice was declared on 11 November and threw his hat in the air in celebration; the following day the family received the telegram stating that his eldest son Edwin had died in France. He died from wounds on 4 November (the last Minchinhampton man to die before the Armistice) at a Casualty Clearing Station and it is likely he was injured in the engagements along the Hindenburg Line. The Ludlow family suffered another tragedy as one of Edwin's sisters, Lily, died in the great flu epidemic.

The Armistice initially ran for thirty days but was regularly renewed until the formal Peace Treaty was signed at Versailles on Saturday, 28 June 1919. A service

The parade in Minchinhampton High Street. (MLHG collection)

of thanksgiving and blessing of the Peace was held on Sunday 6 July in Holy Trinity church. The *Parish Magazine* reported:

> Peace Celebrations were held on Saturday July 19th; the Comrades of the Great War paraded in the Market Square and then marched through the town; Col. Fasken took the salute after presenting Sgt Mgr. J. Cuss with the Military Medal. The wet weather interfered with the full programme for the day, but all demobilised soldiers, sailors and airmen were entertained to dinner in the Market Hall, the children to tea in the National Schools and the wives, widows and mothers of the soldiers and sailors to tea in the Market Hall. The children had their sports in the afternoon but the men's sports were postponed until August Bank Holiday. The bonfire was lighted and the torchlight procession held in spite of the weather.

In the months following the Armistice the thoughts of townsfolk moved to remembrance and commemoration. The *Parish Magazine* of December 1918 states:

> We shall be holding a meeting before long to discuss the subject of a War Memorial to record our thanksgiving to God for victory, and to commemorate those gallant men from this Parish who have fallen during the Great War. It will be felt by many that there should be a Town Memorial, but I am sure that all Church people will agree with me that there MUST be a Memorial of some sort within the Parish Church.

Memorial and Lychgate, Minchinhampton, Glos.

Lychgate in Minchinhampton. (MLHG collection)

In the event both church and town received impressive memorials.

Following the death of both her sons, Mrs Lawrence was supported by the congregation of Holy Trinity church, where she worshipped when in Gloucestershire. In 1918 Mrs Lawrence offered a Calvary in memory of both her sons and all the men who fell in the Great War from Minchinhampton and Box. This monument, designed by Walter Tower, was dedicated in September 1919 and inscribed with forty-seven names of the fallen from the ecclesiastical parish, as well as those of the Lawrence brothers. The Calvary had to be moved from close to the west door of the parish church to its present position in 1973 when the Porch Room was built. Inside Holy Trinity a rood screen, two windows and a restored font were also installed in memory of the fallen.

The first subscription list to be set up was for the Town Memorial, and it was felt by some that the Lower Island buildings should be purchased, renovated and turned into almshouses, or a club for returning soldiers. The Upper Island had been cleared from the lower end of Butt Street in the nineteenth century but Lower Island remained opposite the Market House, bounded by narrow streets, and containing a Church Club, drapers shop and a cottage. Frank Newman was 52 when the Great War broke out, but had served many years in the regular army, finally leaving in 1907 when he became steward of the Church Club in Minchinhampton. The obligation of Reserve Duty for Regulars had an upper age limit but it seems likely that Frank re-enlisted with his old regiment and served with the 3rd (Reserve) Battalion at Maidstone and Chatham. Frank died of a stroke in 1916; he was 54 and his burial in Maidstone Cemetery is recognised by the CWGC. His name is recorded on the memorial which stands on the site of the cottage where he lived in 1911.

In April 1919 Mr T.J. Thompson, who owned the draper's shop, conveyed his property to Col. H.G. Ricardo, the Lord of the Manor, who was acting as agent for the Trustees of the Minchinhampton War Memorial. (The others were the rector and churchwardens, the chairman of the Parish Council and two representatives of the Baptist chapel.) The Church Club, which made up the remaining part of the Island, was conveyed at the same time. The buildings of the Lower Island were very dilapidated, and a decision was taken to remove them and erect a memorial cross in their place. This would have the added benefit of improving the flow of traffic, and opening up the top of the High Street. Sidney Barnsley, one of the celebrated Sapperton Group of craftsmen, was chosen to design the memorial. He is responsible for other crosses in Gloucestershire, notably Poulton, and his brother, Ernest, was the architect of Westfield facing the Great Park, and other local houses.

It was not possible to include the names of the fallen on the cross itself, so these were placed on tablets outside the Market House. To provide room for these the Minchinhampton Fire Brigade received notice to quit in 1919 – for many years their manual engine had been housed behind ornamental iron gates in the undercroft. The engine found a new home in the barn at the back of The Crown public house, and the work on the memorial went ahead. The cross and tablets cost £1,236 13s 3d, raised entirely by public subscription, and included a contribution from the contingent of AFC airmen based at Minchinhampton Aerodrome until 1919.

The dedication of the war memorials throughout the parish is not quite the end of the story of the Great War from Minchinhampton's perspective. The legacy lives on into the twenty-first century. On 28 August 1921 the Comrades came under the auspices of the newly formed British Legion and the local

The Comrades of the Great War in front of the inscribed tablets on the Market House. (MLHG collection)

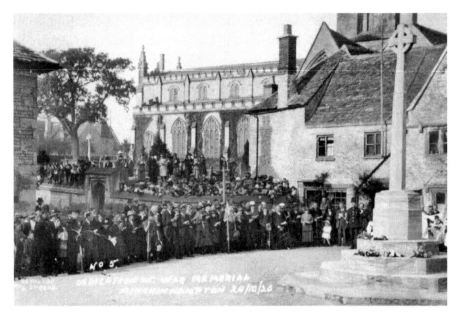

Dedication of the Town Memorial in Minchinhampton on 20 October 1920; the Calvary is in the background. (MLHG collection)

club was formed under the chairmanship of the old Comrades commandant Brigadier General W.H. Tasker. On 9 September 1924, Mr W.F. Woollcombe-Boyce, one of the original members, presented to the branch the vellum book, *Minchin Hampton Parish Record of War Service*, naming all those who had died, been prisoners of war, served overseas or at home. This book was donated in 1994 by the RBL to the Minchinhampton Local History Group, to preserve it for future generations. In 2014, to mark the centenary of the outbreak of the Great War, members of the Local History Group researched the lives of each of the men on the war memorial, completing four volumes which are deposited in Minchinhampton Community Library.

5

MINCHINHAMPTON AERODROME

DIANA WALL

The Australians, like many soldiers from the dominions, fought bravely throughout the Great War and set up their own Air Corps towards the end of the hostilities, looking to the future defence of their shores. In 1917 detachments came to the UK and in January 1918 they set up the First Training Wing of the Australian Flying Corps (AFC), with No. 1 Station (Squadrons 5 and 6) at Minchinhampton (now Aston Down) and No. 2 Station (Squadrons 7 and 8) at Leighterton. Both sites had formerly been open farmland on the Cotswold plateau, and many local workers were employed in the construction.

Aerial view of the aerodrome. (From the collection of the late Malcolm Gay, with permission)

Bessonneau Hangar with an Avro. (From the collection of the late Malcolm Gay, with permission)

Inside the engine shop. (From the collection of the late Malcolm Gay, with permission)

After six weeks' basic training in aeronautics, Morse code and the theory of artillery, and after passing a written examination, the trainees came to Gloucestershire. The novice pilot would 'go solo' after twelve 15-minute dual flights with an instructor then he would have another four hours of solo flight before going on to advanced training – in single-seaters at Minchinhampton and two-seaters at Leighterton. The planes they used were Sopwith Pups and Camels, the S.E.5A and Avro 504. Training was always a risky business, particularly with the Sopwith Camel, which had poor handling characteristics. Sadly, many young men lost their lives during this period – twenty-four are commemorated in St Andrew's parish church at Leighterton and lie in the nearby cemetery. The flimsy machines were often beyond repair, even if the pilot survived a crash.

The first hangars on the fields were of wood and canvas, known as Bessonneau Hangars, but these were eventually replaced by more permanent structures which were large, with light roofs supported by girders. The runways were, of course, grass and there were other buildings such as repair shops, barracks and other facilities for the men.

The Australians became well known locally for their daredevil flying, including dropping into Chavenage House for coffee. The fliers became local celebrities – Captain Les Holden, MC, was the chief instructor at Minchinhampton and he regularly flew his red S.E.5A up the valley from Stroud, turning low over Oakridge and landing at the aerodrome in time for breakfast! The men also put on concert parties and other entertainments for charity, including a concert at Amberley School in aid of a new piano, one in Minchinhampton Market House to raise money for the town war memorial, and far grander, more professional affairs in the Stroud Subscription Rooms – one of which included a mock-up of Minchinhampton aerodrome.

In Spring 1919, as they were preparing to leave the UK, the instructors and men received a visit of inspection from General Sir William Birdwood, Commander-in-Chief of the ANZAC forces. It is believed that the Prince of Wales, later Edward VIII, also visited the aerodrome. After the troops left, the buildings

Captain Les Holden, MC. (From the collection of the late Malcolm Gay, with permission)

Memorial service at Leighterton, 17 November 1918. (Courtesy of the Australian War Memorial)

were abandoned or sold, but, unlike Leighterton, the airfield did not revert to farmland. It was used for air pageants in the 1930s and as the Second World War loomed it was re-opened as Aston Down in October 1938. A few traces remain, in the form of garden outbuildings or bungalows of the administrative centre of the aerodrome. The young men who died during their training for the AFC are not forgotten, however, and every year, on the Sunday nearest to ANZAC Day, an Act of Remembrance is held at Leighterton Cemetery.

> *Oh! You who sleep in Cotswolds' fields,*
> *Sleep sweet – to arise anew;*
> *We caught the torch you threw,*
> *And holding high we kept*
> *The faith with those who died.*
> *We cherish too, the Poppy red*
> *That grows on fields where valour led.*
> *It seems to signal to the skies*
> *That blood of heroes never dies,*
> *But lends a lustre to the red*
> *Of the flower that blooms above the dead.*
> *Fear not that ye have died for naught*
> *We've learned the lesson that ye taught.*

From 'Aussies over the Cotswolds' by James Mc.A Woolley, 1992, an adaptation of Moina Michaels' 1918 poem 'We Shall Keep the Faith'.

6

CHALFORD, FRANCE LYNCH AND BUSSAGE

CAMILLA BOON

The past has the power to surprise us. As soon as war was declared, the Revd Albert Addenbrooke designated the Tuesday evening Eucharist at Christ Church 'a requiem for those who have fallen both on our own side and that of the enemy'. Up the hill at France Lynch, Revd Wade-Evans delivered a sermon in which he pointed out that 'if we were Germans, we would quite as naturally adopt a German attitude, and pray for the success of Germany'. Such even-handedness and lack of jingoism seem startling set against the volatility of those early days of the war, when patriotic crowds were gathering at the railway stations to wave off the troops.

The brutal reality of the war was felt very early in Chalford when on 6 August – less than two days into the war – HMS *Amphion* was sunk by a mine in the North Sea. Two village men, James Hunt and James Rice, were killed. James Hunt, aged 19, had been fostered in a cottage at Clayfields Mill and was an old boy of Christ Church School, which he had recently visited to talk about his life in the navy and travels to countries such as Egypt. James Rice, who was 27, had joined the navy as a boy and risen to the rank of leading signalman in 1910.

At the outbreak of war Chalford was a densely populated semi-industrial village, the various mills along the bottom of the valley providing work for much of the population of Chalford, France Lynch, Bussage and Brownshill. There were several large walking stick factories, flock and shoddy was produced at Iles Mill, and Sevilles Mill manufactured bone objects. There were four schools in the group of villages, a surprising number of pubs, a railway station and many diverse places of worship. The canal was still in everyday use, though

*****|***********|****** *****|***********|*****.

KILLED IN THE AMPHION DISASTER.

Leading Signalman J. W. Rice,   **Seaman J. W. Hunt (A.B.), of**
of Chalford.   **Chalford.**

Both of whom were killed on the Amphion when she struck a German mine in the North Sea on Aug. 5, and sank in 20 minutes. Both were born in Chalford.

*Tribute to James Hunt and James Rice. (*Cheltenham Chronicle and Gloucester Gazette*, courtesy of Gloucestershire Archives)*

it had ceased to be navigable beyond Ashmeads. It was a very sociable area, its inhabitants meeting regularly at religious, musical and cultural events, or playing football and cricket together.

Immediately after the outbreak of the war, many of these groups moved into action, anxious to contribute to the war effort – 'at the present juncture political differences have been sunk' – and the women began knitting and sewing for the troops. So did the schoolchildren, boys included. Large quantities of scarves, mittens and socks were knitted, with bed jackets, pillowcases and 'helpless case shirts' sewn for the Red Cross.

The casualty rate rose slowly to begin with. Soldiers and sailors involved in the fighting at this stage of the war already belonged to the forces, being either active members or past servicemen 'on the Reserve'. Wallace Clissold from Bussage was killed aged 20 during fierce fighting in heavy rain at Soupir, on 14 September. He had just carried his wounded platoon commander to safety. Jack James and Percy Gubbins both died during the First Battle of Ypres (though Percy was not declared dead until July 1915). Ernest Radburn, of Chalford Hill, and Frederick Vick, of Brownshill, serving with the 1st Gloucestershire Regiment, met their ends amidst the freezing mud and sleet at Festubert.

By the end of 1914, several Belgian refugee families had been accommo-dated in France Lynch, their rent either paid by benefactors or provided by the many fundraising activities organised within the local community. Furniture, household effects and food were donated locally. The Jacobs family (a mother and two daughters) lodged initially with a Miss Lamb at Greycot. One of the little girls, Marie, seems to have integrated very quickly into the life of the village – singing the Flemish national anthem at the celebrations when Chalford Hill school won the local schools' gardening shield that November. A Belgian schoolmaster, probably Mr Durine, was given permission to use a classroom at the school to give French lessons. At Christmas, various treats, including coffee, were donated, and an appeal went out for jam, and leeks for soup, the Belgians apparently being 'very fond of them'. Other Belgian families moved into the villages over the next few months, seemingly with little fuss. Once the initial urgency of having to find housing for them had died down, the refugees settled quietly into the community, and there is little subsequent mention of them until they were repatriated at the end of the war – the family from Bliss Mills cottages being sent on their way with a quantity of household goods and tools, intended to help them rebuild their 'desolated home near Liège'.

Chalford saw its fair share of recruitment meetings. The slaughter on the Western Front necessitated a constant supply of new servicemen, but to begin with the authorities wished to avoid conscription. At a meeting on the Green in Chalford Hill in April 1915, accompanied by the band of the 5th Gloucestershires, Mr C.E. Clark JP 'said he was there to perform a most unpleasant duty, that of asking men to join the Forces'. In a rather surreal moment, Mr Carter, the middle-aged Baptist minister, said that if he was a young woman, he would not be seen going out with a young man who had not enlisted. At that time there were about 150 men from the villages in Kitchener's Army, if regular soldiers were included, the total number of local men serving was around 200. A later meeting, held in May on the recreation ground in Chalford Hill, was disrupted by two drunks and a man who revved his motorbike loudly (all were later fined).

It was in 1915 that the sending of parcels to the troops, hitherto an activity undertaken by family and friends, began to be put on a rather more organised footing. There were men, after all, who might not have loved ones. It was also a way of showing the local community's solidarity and care. In Chalford, Miss Mabel Grist, a hugely energetic woman (as the Revd Addenbrooke said, 'when Miss Grist took up anything, she always carried it through') set up a parcels group, based at Halliday's Mill. The initial aim was to send monthly parcels to POWs from the villages – at the time there were two, Private P. Able and Private F. Howell. In October, the *Stroud News* quoted a letter from Private Able, thanking everyone for the parcel and mentioning in particular the playing cards and cigarettes.

The Christmas parcels were on a totally different logistical scale and there were huge cost implications. Funds were raised by whist drives, jumble sales, and – most importantly – concerts. This was an age when people made their own entertainment, and there seems to have been a sufficient balance between those who enjoyed performing comic or sentimental songs, short dramatic sketches, piano solos or dances, and those who were prepared to pay to watch. A typical show towards the end of 1915 raised £9 for the parcels fund. In late 1917, Mr Webster, the headmaster of Chalford Hill School, on the parcels committee, announced that sixty parcels had already been sent 'to men serving with the colours in different parts of the East, and over a hundred had been sent to France and Italy'. Contents included a Christmas pudding, Oxo, cigarettes, cocoa, soap, socks, candles 'and a circular letter of good cheer'.

Eight men from the area died in 1915 and their stories demonstrate how many ways war can kill a man. Albert Clark died in January of meningitis in hospital in Boulogne, aged 24; William Winstone, 22, was killed near Ypres; Christopher Aldum, also 22, was killed during the Battle of Hooge, notorious for the German use of flame throwers. Joseph Ollerenshaw, who at 18 was officially too young to even be at the front, died at Givenchy when a shell landed in his trench. It is in the *Stroud News* report of his memorial service that one can feel the anguish of all these deaths. Reverend Wade-Evans' address is quoted:

Chalford Parcels Group. (Courtesy of Mike Mills)

A page from Chalford VTC notebook.
(Courtesy of the Museum in the Park, Stroud)

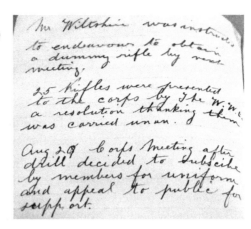

What a cloud had fallen on Chalford Hill when news of that tragedy arrived! How their hearts had gone out to his family, to his mother, to his many friends … Here was a grief so great that words sounded like mockery in its presence.

Two months later, Joseph's cousin, James, a fit young sportsman and trainee schoolmaster, died of pneumonia during training at Epsom, aged 20. Frank Shilham, 20, was a casualty of the Battle of Loos (though he was categorised as 'missing' for two agonising years). Two local men, George Aldridge, 38, and Harry Taysum, 42, died in the hot and thirsty terrain of Gallipoli, whose uncompromising stony landscape was a world away from the wooded hills of home.

In February 1916, after much vacillation, the middle-aged tradesmen who usually took the lead in parish affairs finally managed to organise a meeting to discuss the setting up of a Chalford Volunteer Training Corps (VTC), the Dads' Army of the First World War. They were late doing so – by this time the Bisley VTC had already set up a 'miniature rifle range'. Once established, however, the Chalford VTC met regularly, and its members seem to have been very dedicated. A faded red octavo notebook in Stroud's Museum in the Park contains notes from the early meetings of the group – mainly subscriptions and notes of expenditure.

They carried out regular drills and not particularly strenuous route marches, and were occasionally called on to guard a plane. One came down in Field Place Farm in Bisley in November 1916, and Chalford had the first duty, two hours each, in pairs:

> The night was very unpleasant, and some amusing experiences have been related in regard to the changing of the guard during the night, it being absolutely impossible, owing to the fog, for the men going on duty to locate the machine without shouting to their colleagues.

There were weekend sessions lugging cases of munitions around at Quedgeley Munitions Factory, and training events with other Stroud VTC units. In March 1918, Chalford took part in a mock battle, defending – with Stonehouse VTC – the cricket pavilion against all-comers (the rumour quickly went round that the pavilion contained a barrel of beer). A more sombre duty was attendance at memorial services and military funerals held locally. In the rare cases where a serviceman was buried in the area, they fired a volley over the grave.

There is much news in the local papers of the comings and goings of local servicemen, home on leave or injured. One particularly happy story in September 1916 refers to Private Ashley Young, who had been serving with the Glosters at Delville Wood. He was currently in hospital in Birmingham, recovering from wounds:

> His escape from death was, it transpires, wonderful. At the time he was wounded he was carrying a metal mirror and a Bible in his breast coat pocket. In the operations, however, this had moved somewhat to one side, and the mirror covered the Bible, with the result that the bullet, striking the corner of the mirror and the Bible, was deflected to Young's side, practically scooping the flesh out.

Both objects were soon on display in pride of place in the window of Fred Smart's shop in the High Street – the usual spot for war souvenirs. Ashley Young survived the war and came home to Chalford to marry his sweetheart, May Baughan.

Another Chalford lad, Bernie Gardiner, had just been packed off back home to Belle Vue Terrace, Chalford as underage – he was only 17, but had already seen nine months' service in France, in the thick of many battles, including La Boiselle and 'the great struggle for Pozières Ridge':

> His particular mate was the son of Mr GF Alder of King Street, Stroud, and he was with him when he was killed. He also helped to bury Pte Harry Dowden, another Chalford lad, and at La Boiselle he lost another Chalford friend in the person of Claude Mills, who is now a prisoner of war in Germany.

Bernie re-enlisted the moment he reached 18 in January 1917, but was taken prisoner himself in March 1918:

> He was kept around Metz, and subsequent to the signing of the Armistice was released. He made his way to the Allied lines, and fortunately after wandering about some two days he met the Yankees, who kindly took care of him.

Ashley Young with his father-in-law Mr Baughan, at the foot of Coppice Hill after the war. (Courtesy of Mike Mills)

The tribunals set up to hear appeals against conscription from February 1916 throw light on the life of the villages at the time. Milkmen, farmers, a foreman at the stick factory, engineers – all felt that their talents and energies were better spent on the Home Front. In June, an application was made on behalf of a haulier who worked for the Chalford Water Company, who was described as

> … the only man in Chalford who can efficiently do the work. It was stated that he had charge of two horses, and now that the Canal above Chalford is nearly dry most of the coal has to be hauled by road … if the man was called up they could not supply water to munitions works and other firms.

The application was refused, but the man would not be called up before 31 July. The same month, an application was heard from Sidney Davis of Brownshill, a Chalford pig breeder,

> … who said he had always had a desire to breed and feed pigs and had now been doing it for seven years, and who objected to combatant service. He was a member of the 'Open Brethren', and it was known to two members of the Tribunal that he had strong feelings around the bearing of arms.

He was in fact a member of the Plymouth Brethren and, once it was ascertained that he was happy to provide pigs to the army, he seems to have been left to continue his life in peace.

The year 1916 saw the naval Battle of Jutland and of the Somme and was a time of great loss. The death toll from the Stroud Valley villages was staggering, and everyone would have known somebody affected. Bussage, then a small farming community, was hard hit. Monty Davis, a stonemason, died of meningitis in Salonika in January, aged 23. Albert Clissold, also 23, was killed in the attack on Harrison's Crater in February. William Davis, a career soldier who had joined the Machine Gun Corps, whose family lived near the Ram Inn, died in a Portsmouth hospital in July, aged 30, having had a leg amputated. He is buried in Bussage churchyard. Frederick Stafford had emigrated to Australia before the war, and survived Gallipoli only to be killed near Poznières in July. Eber West was killed in very much the same area in October.

Chalford and France Lynch suffered similarly. Lionel Phipps, a married man and father of three from France Lynch, died on 26 January, two months after being shot in the head. He is buried in Rodborough churchyard. Frank Arnold and Frederick Newman, both in their mid-20s, were casualties of the Battle of Jutland. David Gardiner, who had emigrated to Canada and was fighting with the Canadian forces, was killed on 3 June near Ypres, aged 35. Wallace Phipps, nephew of Lionel, died in a shell blast on 20 June. Heber Webster, youngest son of Frank Webster, died amidst the unimaginable carnage of the Somme, on 3 July, aged 21. Fred Gardiner from Chalford Hill, who had emigrated to Australia where he ran a billiard saloon, fought with the Australians and died on the Somme aged 26. Other village casualties of that campaign were Bill Stevens, 20; Harry Dowden, killed the day after his 17th birthday as he led a prisoner down a communication trench; William Boucher, 23, and David Griffin, 20.

William Morse, an old soldier who had re-enlisted, died of natural causes on 25 August at the age of 46, shortly after he was discharged from service with chronic nephritis and heart disease. He was buried in Christ Church graveyard with military honours. Ernest Young, the son of the nightwatchman at Sevilles Mill was 31 when he was killed on 4 November. Richard Morgan, 26, son of the previous Baptist minister, and Wilfred Harman, 18, who had grown up at the White Horse Inn at the top of Cowcombe Hill, were both killed on 13 November, during the Battle of Ancre, the last phase of the Somme. Willie Workman, a devout young man from France Lynch, died on 6 December at Festubert and Percy Gardiner died near Kut, in Mesopotamia, on 16 December.

There was a tragedy at home, too, when Alice Mary Acton, aged 52, slipped between the train and the platform at Chalford railway station in October whilst seeing her soldier son Robert off to Woolwich after leave. It appeared she had been running alongside the train as it drew out, holding his hand and perhaps trying to kiss him – 'as she was looking into his face she did not see where she was going'. She suffered internal injuries, and though Dr Munden attended immediately and she was taken swiftly to Stroud on the express train (especially stopped for this purpose), she died upon reaching hospital.

The winter of 1916/17 was notorious for its black ice and freezing conditions. There was skating on Toadsmoor Lake, which was fun; however, domestic water pipes froze for weeks on end, which wasn't. People who had kept their wells in working order were thought to be very fortunate.

Private Bert Morse, of the Royal Fusiliers, was described by the local paper as 'a wonderful example of the triumph of modern surgery', having sustained a dreadful wound at Vimy Ridge on Good Friday – 'he managed to lower his head, from which blood flowed freely, and a large piece of shrapnel dropped away. This Morse pluckily secured and kept as a souvenir'. He was unconscious for three days and needed ongoing medical care, but survived the war. Other villagers, too, had been involved in the fighting at Vimy Ridge, especially those who had joined Canadian Regiments. Douglas Webster wrote home to assure his father that he was safe, and mentioned that he had seen Harry Phipps of France Lynch, 'among the Canadians who had captured the German big guns', also Jesse Webb from the village, 'who has come through the fighting unharmed'.

Food controls became tighter and tighter as the war progressed. The main anxieties in 1917 were over wheat, potatoes, sugar, fats and meat. Responsible housekeeping was urged on the nation. In Chalford, communal kitchens were set up 'under the auspices of the National Food Economy Campaign'. The *Stroud News* of 4 May reported:

> Chalford is never slow to take up suggestions which are likely to prove of distinct advantage to the district and the nation at large, and therefore it is not surprising that they have taken the initiative in establishing communal kitchens whereby residents may obtain cooked foods containing as little wheat and flour as possible and where substitutes for potatoes, etc. are used. These kitchens are provided at the Chalford Hill Council School and the Church of England School ... Anyone is invited to visit the schools, the Council on Thursdays and Fridays and the Church on Tuesdays and Wednesdays, to purchase the articles of food provided, which can be bought for the nominal figure of two pence, but they are requested to bring their own 'jugs, basins or baskets'. The cookery lessons at the Schools are being adapted to the requirements of the present food campaign, and the children are assisting as much as possible in the production of the meals provided in the kitchens. The scheme has been in operation since last week, and so far has achieved considerable success ...

Bakers were faced with severe restrictions which included the rather arcane rule that bread could not be sold until it was at least twelve hours old. Horace Stares, who ran the Challenge Bakery in France Lynch, appears to have been the first baker in the area to be prosecuted. He appeared in court in early July, charged with selling bread less than twelve hours old to two customers. In his defence, he stated that he had taken the bread out of the oven at 5 a.m., and had instructed his son, who acted as delivery boy, not to take it out till after school, which finished at 4 p.m. – 'he quite thought the boy would have his tea before going with it, but instead of doing so he delivered it at once'. It had only been sold forty minutes early. Mr Stares was let off, having been made an example of.

When the vicar of Christ Church, Revd Addenbrooke, offered himself to the bishop for war work, he almost certainly had not envisaged being assigned to what the bishop himself described as an 'experimental' position: that of chaplain to the munitions workers at Quedgeley Filling Factory. Nor did the job seem to play to his strengths. A gentle and self-doubting man, he obviously found the urban working-class women among his flock rather shocking:

> There are those thousands of quite independent girls and women living in the city, earning more money than they ever had before and spending it, for I am told very few save anything … (Christ Church parish magazine)

He was at a loss as to what to do, as most workers were not keen to attend conventional services, but thought creatively, begging a piano for the canteen so he could organise a choir, and arranging outings. His behind-the-scenes tours of Gloucester Cathedral were extremely popular. Another trip involved a picnic at Highnam, where they gathered flowers and came across the composer Sir Hubert Parry, who invited them to his house. However, Addenbrooke was 'often greatly discouraged and in despair', and kept petitioning the bishop to be allowed home. The bishop, apparently feeling that good work was being done, made him stay the full year, April 1917 until April 1918.

In June, *Stroud News* reported that 'considerable excitement' was felt at 'the arrival in an aeroplane of Flight Lieutenant Wilfred Selwyn, who landed in a field at Manor Farm … the field is situated to the north of Frith Wood, and the gallant Lieutenant, who arrived on a visit to his parents at Toadsmoor, was quickly the centre of a large and admiring crowd …' He was in the process of conveying the new aircraft from the Midlands to Wiltshire, and took off again at 4.30 p.m., 'making a graceful and perfect rise from the earth'.

Towards the end of summer 1917, there were anxieties about fuel supplies – 'there was practically a coal famine in Chalford'. This was not simply because

View along the canal at Chalford, looking towards Smart's Wharf. (Courtesy of Mike Mills)

of lack of supply (so many miners having joined up, and stocks being diverted to the war effort), but also logistical problems transporting the coal up the canal because so many bargees had been conscripted. James Smart, the principal coal merchant in the village, was also chairman of the Parish Council and well-placed to lobby the authorities. He had had six barges, but was reduced to two working, and the mate of one of those had just been called up.

In November, there was disquiet about the state of the road between St Mary's and the main village, which had been churned up by the heavy traffic involved in the construction of 'a new aerodrome on the high level above Cowcombe Hill Road':

> The residents have taken the inconvenience caused by the bad roads to be one of the results of the war, but they are nevertheless glad that attention is at last being given to the matter.

The casualty list for 1917 involves all sorts and conditions of men, and is testimony to the arbitrary nature of war. The savage fighting and nightmare conditions of Passchendaele, which officially began on 31 July (but involved previous preparation), claimed by far the greatest proportion of this year's dead, but others met their end in the Holy Land and France, or died of illness. Sidney Phelps, 29, serving with the Canadians, died of nephritis in hospital in France in February; Sidney Gubbins, not passed fit enough for overseas service, died while serving on Home Defence duties, aged 23, in Walton-on-the-Naze.

Ernest Davis, an enthusiastic member of the Chalford band, who had been so keen to join up underage that he tried three different recruiting offices before he found one that would take him, was killed in Salonika at 20. Frank Wear, a father of four, died in the Battle for Vimy Ridge, aged 31. Charlie Pidgeon, a hugely loved young man, 'one of the most cheerful men in the Battalion', was killed at Messines Ridge on 7 June aged 22. Albert Stevens, who had worked in James Smart's stable, died the same day, of typhoid in France. Albert Goodfield, from Frampton Mansell, died of wounds sustained during the build up to Passchendaele, aged 18. Ernest Kirby, 28, a gardener, was killed a few days before his friend and fellow Grenadier Guardsman Fred Couldrey, a coal merchant, 32, in July. Both these men had appealed to the tribunals unsuccessfully, Ernest on the grounds that he was growing vegetables for the nation at Hind's nursery, Fred because he was running the family coal merchants. They were at Passchendaele, which also claimed the lives of 31-year-old Percy Tyler, a decorator, and George Herbert, a stick worker with 'a quiet and unassuming manner', also 31. Bertie Smith was killed by a grenade in France, aged 22. Charles Hemmings met his end at Langemarck, another victim of Passchendaele. Francis Young, soon after joining up, was found to have TB, 'aggravated by but not caused by military service'. He died aged 31 in hospital in Blackpool and is buried in France Lynch, under a War Graves headstone. Harry Pincott from Bussage, a signaller who had enlisted early in the war and had been awarded the Military Medal, died on 30 September of wounds received at Passchendaele. Ten days later, Arthur Mayo, who had worked as a butler at Harescombe Grange, was killed there, aged 37. The same month, Edwin Overbury, an 'extremely cheerful' Chalford postman working at Passchendaele as a stretcher-bearer, died aged 34. In another part of the conflict entirely, Hywel Morgan, 33, nicknamed 'Smiler', whose brother Richard had been killed in 1916, died in fighting around Jerusalem. Back at Passchendaele, Charles Herbert, brother of George and close friend of Ernest Kirby and Fred Couldrey, went missing on 1 December. Captain of the local cricket and football teams, an intensely charismatic and energetic man, his death sent shockwaves around the whole Stroud district. Frederick King, another Guardsman, was killed in the same attack. Francis Young died at Cambrai, and Maurice Goodship, 19, was killed, like Hywel Morgan, near Jerusalem. Gilbert Damsell, a stretcher-bearer who received a Military Medal 'for helping to estab-lish a First Aid Post, collecting wounded on the field and dressing them under heavy shell fire', received a fatal wound in the head at Passchendaele, and died aged 25 on 21 December.

As 1918 dawned, expectations of the New Year were not high. The war seemed to have been going on for ever. Food controls were beginning to morph into rationing; the villages were denuded of most of their young and middle-aged men. Many households dreaded the arrival of a letter or telegram bearing bad news.

The authorities were encouraging pig-keeping, though Chalford Parish Council was ambiguous about it, feeling that there would be insufficient left-overs to feed the animals with. However, they expressed solidarity with a parishioner who had received a letter of complaint,

> ... about him keeping pigs and he understood this was by a person who had come to Chalford to get away from the air-raids. The sty had been in the same place for 20 years, and pigs had been fattened there continually. The Council thought the parishioner should not be interfered with, particularly at such a time as this.

The fine spring and early summer weather brought large numbers of curious visitors through Chalford to see the aerodrome at Minchinhampton. They came by railcar (though the Sunday service was suspended from 1 April), on bicycles and on foot, toiling up Cowcombe Hill. At Whitsun, 'the roads were hard and dusty, which made the ascent from the valley in brilliant sunshine a rather exhausting performance'. The *Stroud News* commented that the aerodrome was 'the chief outdoor attraction in the locality'.

The aerodrome also provided welcome employment to the area. A rare glimpse of local women's contribution is offered in two accounts from the local papers. In its issue of 29 March, the *Stroud Journal* relates:

> The newly-formed branch of the Women's Federation, composed chiefly of workers from the aerodrome, held their first meeting at the Parish Rooms, Chalford, on Wednesday evening in the last week, under the presidency of Miss Codrington. As a result of the proceedings, the wishes of the members have been satisfactorily met by the contractor. The Federation will be pleased to welcome any additional women workers from the locality.

The women were 'navvying', 'levelling ground, assisting the builders and filling in the sub-soil for water main trench'. When, within a month (whether or not as a result of their union-style activities), forty women were laid off without the weeks' notice (or the pay in lieu) to which they were entitled, Miss Codrington was there fighting the cause. At a tribunal held in Stroud, she made the case for the female workers very cogently, and the payment of the outstanding 34s was agreed.

Women's contribution to the war is imperfectly recorded – only visible by accident. There are two exquisite photographs of Sally and Edith Mills, from

Edith Mills (later Baglin) working at T.H. & J. Daniels. (Courtesy of Mike Mills)

Chalford, as they concentrate on their engineering work, making shell casings, at T.H. & J. Daniels.

Dorothy Clissold, of Bussage, whose brother Wallace had been killed in 1914, went out to France as a cook with Queen Mary's Army Auxiliary Corps. The names of several other local women can be found in the Red Cross records.

In June, the Chalford Woodworking Company acquired the premises formerly belonging to Messrs Clark Bros, Millers – 'the interior is being dismantled, and we understand the place is to be equipped with a special process for the manufacture of parts of air-craft …'

Flu swept through the area in the autumn of 1918. On 18 October, the *Stroud News* reported that 'the influenza epidemic is very severe in the Chalford district, and business and trade is only carried out with great difficulty. Unfortunately, there have been two or three deaths'. These included Ada Jellyman, only 21, a teacher at France Lynch School, who lived with her parents at the Railway Inn, Brownshill. She had been in good health on Friday, but died on the Sunday night.

The end of the war, when it finally came, was signalled by 'a prolonged blast on the hooter at Bliss Mills'. There was a general air of euphoria:

Flags were displayed, the bells at the Parish Church were rung, and the firing of cannon from Mr James Smart's Wharf and elsewhere materially helped to spread the glad tidings … Business was entirely suspended 'on all fronts' and sane jollity reigned supreme to a late hour at night.

The schools were closed for the rest of the day, and the churches held thanks-giving services.

The final year of desperate, vicious fighting left a terrible toll. Christopher Philpotts, a stick worker from France Lynch, died aged 19 in January. His brother Harry, who had emigrated to Canada, was killed in October at the age of 25 – 'a good soldier, a great personality'. Louis Reginald Pearce, 26, served in Egypt where he developed the debilitating illness which caused his death, after much suffering, in February. He is buried in the Tabernacle graveyard. Archie Hemmings (whose brother had been killed in 1917) met his death in the German Spring offensive. He was 29. Albert Pegler, 21, died when the SS *Lady Cory White* was torpedoed in the English Channel. Francis Webb, aged 35, initially rejected for the army because of short sight, faded from view in April 1918, when his previously frequent letters home dried up. He was not declared dead until June 1919. Terrance Dean, who was 22, had come close to death on several occasions, but his luck finally ran out in April 1918 near Messines, where Maurice Baker also died, as did Archie Baker. Thomas Smart died of meningitis while home on leave visiting his dying mother. He lies in France Lynch churchyard. Charley Shergold was only 18 when he died of wounds after a mere month at the front. Fred Matthews, who had moved to Coventry and married there, died aged 30, somewhere on the Western Front in July.

Drummer Sidney Halliday had emigrated to Canada and served with the Winnipeg Grenadiers. He was killed at Hallu in August, aged 22. His body was not recovered until 2006, when the remains of eight Canadian soldiers were discovered in the back garden of a newly built house. Sidney's identity was finally revealed by a love token, a locket containing the initials of his sweetheart Lizzie, and confirmed by analysis of his teeth. He was reinterred in the cemetery at Caix in 2015.

Eddie Hook had also emigrated, but to New Zealand. He joined up there and died in the Battle of Amiens, aged 35. Albert Griffin, a principled young Baptist 'impelled by duty', badly wounded earlier in the conflict, returned to the front and perished aged 28 on the Somme. Another devout Baptist and temperance worker, Albert King, who was a cabinet maker, died in hospital in Northumberland, probably from the strain on his heart of active service, aged 29. He was buried at Christ Church. Percy Mills was killed at the age of 19; Joseph Ward, 33, left a wife and two small daughters when he was killed at Bourlon Wood – the same fighting that claimed the life of Clifford Brazneill, aged 21 and Chester Goodfield (whose brother Albert had been killed in 1917). Edward Cook was 21 when he died at St Quentin Canal.

Three servicemen were buried in France Lynch churchyard within eight days of each other in October and November. Poor Rupert Gardiner was another lad to die while training, at the age of 18, only three months after enlisting. Frank Damsell also never served overseas, but died at the age of 20. The vicar noted that both these men died of influenza. The third soldier, Wilfred Hale, died of a head injury aged 27 on 30 October. Percy Hughes died while a prisoner of war, on 4 November. Ernest Halliday was another victim of the influenza. He died on 8 November, aged 29, in Salonika.

The end of hostilities did not mean an end to the deaths of servicemen. William Creed, based in France, probably on clearance work, died of TB in hospital in Boulogne in February 1919. Alexander Clissold died of the after-effects of a head wound received in August 1917, having struggled on until April 1919. Trevor Webster, oldest son of the Chalford Hill headmaster, was killed in a cycling accident shortly before he should have returned to Canada, in August. Victor Chapman, a baker, came home to his wife Milly on Rack Hill suffering from lung problems, having been gassed. He died in November 1919.

There never seems to have been any discussion about the form of Chalford's war memorial: it was always going to be a Wayside Calvary like those in France, which serving soldiers bore witness seemed to survive even when the rest of a village had been annihilated in the fighting. A symbol of triumph over the destruction of war, but also an image of suffering, must have seemed supremely appropriate.

The newly unveiled war memorial in 1920. From right to left: Lionel Cottle, Revd Addenbrooke, Flaxman Cottle and Omar Cottle. (Courtesy of Christ Church, Chalford)

In November 1919, a year after the Armistice was announced, Omar Cottle, a local stonemason, submitted a maquette of his figure of the crucified Christ. This was unanimously admired, indeed, all were 'very delighted to think this important piece of work is to be carried out entirely by local men and we doubt if there will be many villages in England, where the memorial to those who have died will be the work of men in the place.' It was estimated the figure would cost in the region of £208. Fundraising was immediately stepped up. It was hoped that those who wished to commemorate their dead on the monument would contribute 7s, to cover the cost of carving the Christian name and surname on the base (though no one would be excluded through inability to pay).

Things moved swiftly: by December 1919, a stone big enough for the cross and figure had been obtained and was in the process of being roughly shaped at the quarry. By January, 'the work of carving the figure is actually in hand and may be seen in Mr Cottle's workshop at St Mary's'. Money poured in and donations are meticulously detailed in the parish magazines. There were sixty-four names by the time the memorial was dedicated, on 6 June 1920, in what was obviously an emotional service.

There was a Requiem Eucharist in memory of those who died – whose names were read out at the altar – followed by a muffled peal on the bells and at 2.30 p.m. the Comrades of the Great War (the survivors) marched to the memorial, led by the Chalford Band, who gave their services for free. Relatives of the dead had precedence and were admitted by ticket into the roped-off area around the memorial. Dr Edwards, who had been chosen by the ex-servicemen, unveiled the figure, and prayers were said for the dead and for the bereaved. The bishop preached and the Last Post was sounded.

7

THE WOODCHESTER WAYSIDE CROSS

'THE FIRST WAR MEMORIAL'

PHILIP GOODWIN

Over the last two years there have been extensive efforts made to restore a remarkable monument at Inchbrook. Built below the Dominican Priory church between July 1916 and May 1917 the Wayside Cross at Woodchester was probably the first war memorial in the country, and during the Great War people attended ceremonies there in their thousands – 2-3,000 people were at the opening ceremony on 3 June 1917, and perhaps up to 10,000 people were at the first Remembrance Sunday held here on 4 August 1918, the fourth anniversary of the outbreak of war. There had been a few plaques in private chapels for the Crimean and Boer Wars, but nothing serving a whole town or district.

Two events happened in 1914 leading to its construction. Firstly a new prior, Father Hugh Pope, was appointed to the Dominicans at Woodchester. He led the novices, the ordained and the lay members of the community. Secondly a shot was fired in Sarajevo which led to the enlistment of hundreds of Stroud men, including several members of the priory, to fight for King and country. Father Pope gave sermons outlining the plight of occupied Belgium and encouraging men to enlist to fight in the cause of justice and freedom. From August 1914 they began to be brought home injured or dead. In 1914 there was shock that a single shot could lead to such sacrifice; in 1915 the horror grew as it became apparent that the war would not be over soon, and that the stalemate of the trenches of the

The Wayside Cross, Woodchester. (Courtesy of Gloucestershire Archives)

Father Hugh Pope O.P., prior of Woodchester. (Courtesy of Gloucestershire Archives)

Western Front would continue to bring news of escalating casualties. Father Pope was very aware of the grief felt by himself and the people of the Stroud Valleys. Many were members of his congregation.

The idea to build a monument to pay tribute to those who had sacrificed their lives in the Great War was first conceived by the prior, influenced by his parishioners, including Lady Mostyn of Benwell House who had lost her nephew Maurice Dease in August 1914, the first VC of the war. Perhaps it was the loss in October 1914 of George Archer Shee, another parishioner, or the loss of Jack Quinn, the fostered garden boy at the priory, who had been so keen to enlist but who had been killed aged just 20.

The idea of setting up a big cross in memory of those who had fallen in the war was first thrown out towards the end of 1915. At first it was intended merely for those who were members of the congregation at the Monastery Church. But it was soon felt that this idea would make a far wider appeal than was at first anticipated, for men of all classes and faiths had fallen. Those who mourned their loss and realised the immensity of the sacrifice made by these men and by those who gave them for the cause of freedom and humanity were anxious to have their names perpetuated.

Father Pope felt it would be too exclusive to restrict such a memorial to the fallen of his parish. He had genuine sympathy for all the grieving families in the Stroud district, 'his neighbours', and wanted to extend the availability of a memorial to all who had lost someone, rich and poor, 'for all classes and creeds'. As he wrote in his proposal issued in early 1916:

> These heroes … who hail from our villages and hamlets, whom we have known and talked with in the days before the war when they went out with a handshake and their place knew them no more – these simple but great hearted men have made the great sacrifice and have known that they were making it. They have claimed kinship with the Prince of Peace.

It was a picture of a forlorn soldier sitting at the base of a Wayside Cross in a devastated French town that inspired him to want similar as a memorial in Stroud. He was inspired by the soldier's picture and the message of redemption it implied, a symbol of both Christ's sacrifice and the redemption afforded by that sacrifice. Although adjacent to their priory and planned by their prior, it did become a monument for all. People gave subscriptions generously. The grieving did not have to subscribe; they had only to make the request and the name would be added. There were no other memorials in the country for people to honour their men and to have remembrance. At the end of the war Father

Pope thought that there would be about 150 names. Eventually 140 names were inscribed on twelve Portland stone plaques.

Donations were asked for in the spring of 1916. On 4 July he wrote that two people in particular had been generous; Mr Workman, who owned the wood yard in Woodchester and several of whose workers, including Walter Fruin, were killed in the war, provided the wood. Mr Brown, who today owns the same wood yard, has given the wood for the restoration. Mr Leigh, who owned Woodchester mansion, provided the stone. Father Pope had a budget and the plan was formalised. He wrote on 28 July 1916 that the requisite £100 had been already collected and that the work had been put in the hands of the sculptor. We can, therefore, safely date the start of the memorial to July or August 1916. Father Pope expected the cross to be completed quickly but found that so many sculptors were at the front that delays became inevitable. He himself drew up a design but was unhappy with it. Mr Falconer of Amberley, an experienced architect, told him that if he needed help to 'knock on his door' and it is his design that we see today.

Father Pope's plan brought immediate reaction. Several letters were written to the *Stroud News*, particularly from the vicars of Woodchester and Stroud, who saw the new memorial as a Catholic monument, disliked the public exposure of the figure of Christ and saw the building of a memorial in a public place as

The Wayside Cross in early 1917. (Courtesy of Gloucestershire Archives)

their prerogative. They saw the matter as coming under their domain. There was great rivalry and perhaps some bigotry involved in some of the letters published in the *Stroud News*. This view was not shared by any other correspondents such as the minister for Nailsworth, Revd Frank Smyther, or 'A Soldier', writing to the newspaper from the trenches, who saw it as entirely appropriate to honour those who had made the ultimate sacrifice with a depiction of Christ. The

Dedication of the Wayside Cross, 3 June 1917. (Courtesy of Gloucestershire Archives)

objections were overcome by general support from the people of Stroud who wanted it and were encouraged in their support by the news that several of the Dominican community were fighting for the Allies in the trenches of France.

The prior gave a sizeable strip of the meadows bordering the road that was later to be the A46, and in May 1917 Messrs Newman and Hender straightened and greatly widened the road to accommodate the hundreds expected to attend the dedication ceremony on 3 June 1917. In the event, 2-3000 came to hear the dedication by the Archbishop of Clifton and to lay flowers on the cross. On the day the life-size figure of Christ coming from London by train never arrived. At the last hour the prior ordered that another figure that had been given to the Priory by William Gladstone's sister some years previously was to be a substitute, and the ceremony went ahead.

The ceremony was held on Sunday evening. The central figures were the Right Revd Dr Burton, Roman Catholic Bishop of Clifton, the Revd Hugh Pope, and other priests who entered the field from the monastery promptly on the stroke of 6.30. They were preceded by children and men carrying ornate banners. Members of the Stroud and Nailsworth Companies of the 4th Gloucesters attended under the command of Major C.A. Hope, three captains and three lieutenants. The Boy Scouts of Stroud and district formed a cordon around the cross outside the volunteers who acted as guard of honour.

The names were painted on in black and later inscribed:

THIS WAYSIDE CROSS
WAS ERECTED ON JUNE 3, 1917 BY THE
DOMINICAN FATHERS
OF WOODCHESTER
WITH THE GENEROUS ASSISTANCE OF
ALL CLASSES AND CREEDS FROM THE
DISTRICT AND ALL PARTS OF THE
EMPIRE IN MEMORY OF THOSE WHO GAVE
THEIR LIVES IN THE CAUSE OF FREEDOM IN
THE GREAT WAR
1914-1918

The Foundation Stone gives the date of the opening rather than that of the erection.

If the vast crowds that turned out on 3 June 1917 were unexpected, then that surprise was exceeded by the even greater number who came to the first ever Remembrance Sunday, held on 4 August 1918, the fourth anniversary of the outbreak of the war, as well as being Trinity Sunday and St Dominic's Day:

… it would be hard to recall any function like it … it will be obvious to say that as far as the eye could reach, all along the Bath Road, up the hillside to the Common, and right up to the monastery church itself, stretched a crowd such as the neighbourhood has never seen. For even last year, when this Cross was consecrated by Bishop Burton, and a crowd that experienced people estimated as ten thousand had assembled, there was not such an assemblage as on Sunday.

The sermon was given by Cardinal Bourne, who had arrived from London by train. The *Stroud News* had explained to those who asked what a cardinal was. He spoke at length on the progress of the war, which by this time was almost won, and gave thanks to God, to those who had died, to those who had lost their menfolk, and to those who had prayed.

From the 1920s until 2014 there came a slow deterioration of the memorial. Remembrance was carried out at town and village memorials. By the 1960s the Wayside Cross had become overgrown and neglected. From the 1980s some people, notably Brendan Shiner, took an interest in it and began to care for it, the first war memorial of the Great War in the area. Notable casualties include Maurice Dease VC; George Archer-Shee, 'the Winslow Boy'; William Jennings, the son of the vicar of Kings Stanley, whose rescue from the battlefield earned

Remembrance Sunday, 4 August 1918. (Courtesy of Gloucestershire Archives)

The Wayside Cross in November 2014, following extensive restoration work. (Author's photo)

Tom Turrall the VC; and Richard Raymond-Barker, the seventy-ninth pilot shot down by the Red Baron. The Red Baron himself was killed the next day.

The monument received extensive restoration work in 2014. Thanks must be given particularly to Renishaws plc, Dennis Brown wood yards, Mr James Chamberlain, The Stuart Singers, Mr Alan Hawkins, the mason, and the many others who have given time and money for its restoration. The Wayside Cross has become once again an impressive monument; a fitting memorial to the heroes of Stroud and beyond who, 100 years ago, knowingly made the ultimate sacrifice. It is also a tribute to the steadfast efforts of the Dominican Prior, Father Hugh Pope, the first to conceive of a war memorial and to have the conviction to carry the project to completion.

8

WOODCHESTER

BARBARA WARNES

When the census was taken on the night of 2 April 1911, Woodchester, a parish with an area of 1,206 acres, had a population of 831 in 189 households. Surprisingly, there were far more female residents than male – 468 to 363. Of the males, approximately 130 were aged between 13 and 36, eligible to be conscripted in 1916 (when they would all have reached 18).

At the declaration of war, Woodchester was a normal village with three churches, several public houses and shops and a considerable amount of industry in the valley. The new Anglican church was just over 50 years old and apparently there had been some concern about the validity of marriages taking place since its opening. The *Western Daily Press* reported:

> A Bill was introduced into the House of Commons to confirm a provisional order legalising marriages up to October 15th 1914. Questions have arisen as to whether these new churches, which were built in substitution for old ones, were legally authorised for the solemnisation of marriages, and this Bill will make legal all such marriages that have taken place in the churches. The clergymen who have solemnised the marriages will be released from any penalties that they may have incurred.

A new rector, Revd George Edward Watton, had been recently appointed. Father Hugh Pope had come to the monastery and the Baptist church was without a pastor (Revd A.T. Maddocks from Cardiff would arrive shortly). The old Elizabethan rectory and tithe barn at the junction of Church Lane and Selsley Road had just been demolished and rebuilding begun. A progress report before

Woodchester School, 1914. The man on the left of the picture is thought to be the headmaster, George Home Ricketts. (Bill Brunt collection)

the Bank Holiday weekend stated that the walls were about 3 feet high, building would take longer than expected and cost more as the price of timber rose. Just one of the effects of the war. The school in North Woodchester reopened for the autumn term without its headmaster; George Home Ricketts had already been called up for active service.

The Defence of the Realm Act (DORA), passed on 8 August 1914, among other things imposed restrictions on the pubs and alehouses. Opening times and alcohol strength were reduced, while it also became an offence to buy drinks for others.

In September, Belgian refugees were housed at Summerwells, children from an orphanage in Ghent being taken in by the nuns at the Franciscan Convent at the southern end of the village.

The first man recorded on the Woodchester War Memorial, both alphabetically and chronologically, is Lieutenant George Archer-Shee of the South Staffordshire Regiment, a career soldier. He is known to many throughout the world but his name will only be recognised by a few. The story of his time at Osborne Naval College on the Isle of Wight, where he was accused of stealing a postal order, has been preserved in Terence Rattigan's play *The Winslow Boy*. He was reported missing on 31 October 1914 at the First Battle of Ypres, aged 19. His mother spent many months trying to find out what had happened to him before accepting his death. Although the congregation of the Priory church would have known, many of the residents of Woodchester may not have

North Woodchester Post Office. The postmistress was Mrs Sarah Cordwell, wife of builder Edward Cordwell. Their son, Charles Edward, served with the Dragoon Guards and was awarded the Distinguished Conduct Medal in January 1915. (Bill Brunt collection)

been aware of this casualty. Helen Archer-Shee had only recently moved into a house called Littleholme (now Winslow House) on Atcombe Road in South Woodchester and as George was already serving in the army it is not known how much time, if any, he spent in the village. His 14-year-old sister, Helen, had died in 1913 of meningitis and is buried in the churchyard at the Priory church.

At a Parish Council meeting on 11 January 1915, a letter was read from the Weekly Dispatch offering a medallion to the village who sent the most men to join HM Forces during the 'present crisis'. Mr Woodward (the baker in South Woodchester High Street) kindly offered to put this up in his shop window, so that the public could see the offer. There is no indication of the public's view of the matter or what it did for recruitment!

The war impacted on all sections of the community, not only those called upon to fight. In June, the *Cheltenham Chronicle* reported that the Monastery had already sent at least six Fathers with some connection to Woodchester to the front – one of whom had survived the terrible rail crash at Quintinshill. More were to follow. They served bravely as army chaplains working both close to the trenches and in Casualty Clearing Stations. At least two were awarded the Military Cross for conspicuous gallantry.

In July of the same year, a committee was formed for the purpose of National Registration and an attempt was made to form a roll of men willing to serve as a Voluntary Training Corps.

By autumn, Woodchester was to discover the reality of war. Edgar Miles of the Glosters was returned from the Balkans suffering from dysentery and dehydration, and died in Netley Military Hospital in Hampshire on 3 October, aged 23.

On the 13th of the same month, 19-year-old William Albert Rigsby, of Station Hill, was killed in action at Loos serving with the Glosters. He was the son of the village postman. Two days later, on the 15th, 30-year-old Walter William Beard of the Cross died of wounds in hospital in France. He was an Acting Corporal in the Royal Engineers and left behind a wife and young family. The Beards were umbrella stick manufacturers. These were men known by many in the village and their loss would have been widely felt.

Meanwhile, a petition from a number of parishioners was received by the Parish Council asking them to obtain a better supply of water at the spring near the Baptist chapel in South Woodchester. By March the following year Mr Harding had collected £10 5s, which he handed over to the clerk in April for repairs.

The Police Courts continued as normal in Stroud and in January 1916, a 13-year-old boy from Mill Cottages (near Woodchester Mill – the 'Piano

The Cross in South Woodchester, where the Beard family lived. (Bill Brunt collection)

Works') was charged with stealing a larch pole valued at 2*s* from the ruins of Rodborough Manor. The chairman of the magistrates, being mainly concerned with parents not punishing their children adequately, dismissed the case against the boy and ordered the father to pay 2*s* for the value of the pole and 2*s* costs.

There had been a brief respite in bad news from the front and the next death may only have lightly touched the village. Walter Alfred Cox was an Indian tea planter, descended from a Painswick family, who came over from Travancore and enlisted, first in the King's Royal Rifles but later being transferred to the Machine Gun Corps. However, the battlefield was not to claim him – he died of malaria in April 1916, aged 39, in Belton Park Military Hospital in Grantham, Lincolnshire without firing a shot in anger. He was buried in St Mary's church-yard and remembered with an inscription on the reverse of his aunt's headstone. A 'war grave' stone has since been added.

However, the death of 20-year-old Walter William John Fruin of the Glosters, formerly of Convent Lane, on the 30 April, would not have passed unnoticed. He died of wounds near Abbeville. He had lived all his life in the village, work-ing at Henry Workman's Timber Yard, and went to France in August 1915 with Albert Rigsby.

Sadly, on 3 July, Woodchester was shaken by the news that Frederick Percy Click, aged 21, and Wilfred James Brinkworth, aged 22, both of the Glosters, were killed in the early stages of the Battle of the Somme. A memorial service for them was held at the Baptist church. Then on the 21st, 30-year-old George Home Ricketts, also of the Glosters, was killed at Pozières. He was a man known to many families in the village, being headmaster of the school in North Woodchester. He was awarded a Military Medal posthumously for an act of gallantry not associated with his death. The school logbook records:

> This week a photograph of Mr G H Ricketts, Headmaster of this school 1911 to 1916, was placed in the schoolroom to his memory. He gave his life for King and Country at the Battle of the Somme July 21st 1916. It is with deep regret we have to record his death for he was an earnest and devoted Master of this School.

A further sum of £1 15*s* had been collected towards the expense of the spring in South Woodchester, leaving a deficiency of 14*s*; this was generously donated by the chairman of the Parish Council, Henry Workman.

On 22 July, the *Cheltenham Chronicle* reported on an inquest recently held on the death in Stroud Hospital of Robert Henry Evans from tetanus. The young man, who lived with his parents in Inchbrook, worked for United Brassfounders (Newman Hender) in Woodchester. A week before his death, he had had three

South Woodchester High Street, home of many men who served in the Great War. (Bill Brunt collection)

teeth extracted but this did not seem to have troubled him. Dr Davies, who examined the body, said he could only find a small wound on a finger of the right hand and it was very difficult to say whether this or the use of a hypodermic needle was the origin of the disease.

In August, there was happier news from Woodchester. The *Stroud News* reported:

> The Friends of Rifleman Harry Clift of the King's Royal Rifles will be pleased to hear he is at his charming little Woodchester home after fifteen weeks in hospital suffering from shell shock. He joined the colours at the outbreak of war and was at the front for nearly 12 months. His brother Private W. Clift of the Gloucesters, who was badly wounded at Loos, is also home on leave and doing well.

There was also a touch of normality:

> Mr H Brinkworth, caretaker of Woodchester Mills, possesses a hen which on Sunday morning laid an egg 6oz in weight and containing 3 yokes [*sic*]. The following morning, the same hen laid an egg which contained 2 yokes.

The year 1916 had still not finished with Woodchester. The Rigsby family were hit once again as news was received that Frederick Ernest (William Albert's brother) had been killed by a shell at Thiepval during the Battle of the Somme on 25 October. He was 21 and serving with the Glosters. Before the war, he worked for Perkins and Marmont at Frogmarsh Mill.

Conscription had been introduced in 1916, all men between the ages of 18 and 41 being eligible for call up. However, it was possible to apply for exemption and many employers, in an attempt to hold on to their workforce, did just that but of course the military also appealed. In September 1917, the *Gloucester Journal* reported that a firm of piano manufacturers in Woodchester answered the appeal of the military against exemption granted to the proprietor of the business (28, married, A), and two workers (38, married, C2 and 34, married, C1). A, C1 and C2 were categories of 'fitness':

A   Able to march, see to shoot, hear well and stand active service conditions.
C   Free from serious organic diseases, able to stand service in garrisons at home.
C1   Able to march 5 miles, see to shoot with glasses, and hear well.
C2   Able to walk 5 miles, see and hear sufficiently for ordinary purposes.

It was stated that a good deal of munition work was being done. The tribunal confirmed the decision of the local tribunal granting exemption in each case to the end of the year.

For nine months the village had had respite from news of deaths, before Ernest Wear, a house decorator from Bospin Lane, was killed in action at Passchendaele, during the Third Battle of Ypres on 1 August 1917, aged 35. He had enlisted in the Glosters and been transferred to the Royal Berkshire Regiment. He left a wife and young son.

Also in October, on the 26th, 19-year-old Maurice John Howell from Mill Cottages was reported missing at Passchendaele, while serving with the Devonshire Regiment.

The year was still not over. Arthur Kirby of the Glosters, was wounded and taken prisoner at the Battle of Cambrai on 2 December. He died of his wounds on the 11th, aged 19. He had lived in Woodchester, in or around Selsley Road, all his life and worked at Henry Workman's Timber Yard.

Henry John Wager, aged 25, a baker from Church Road, died of wounds on 25 April 1918 whilst serving with the Rifle Brigade in France. He had commenced his service in the Royal Army Service Corps where his number suggests he was engaged in 'Supply' in a labouring capacity – probably moving stores. He arrived in France in 1915, possibly part of a draft to assist in the trenches as they 'required an enormous amount of work'. He is remembered in St Mary's churchyard on the gravestone of his sister.

Children are children everywhere and the war did not change this. The headmaster recorded the following in the school logbook in July.

On arriving at the school on Monday morning, I found a good deal of marking had been placed on the school walls, some reflecting on the staff and other disgraceful words. I called the Managers' attention to this and asked that the perpetrators should be found and punished as it will interfere if allowed to pass unnoticed with the discipline of the school.

18th July 1918
The boy wrote an apology and expressed his regret for what he had written on the school walls respecting the staff and this was accepted and further proceedings stayed.

A 16-year-old boy from South Woodchester appeared at Nailsworth Petty Sessions for using a catapult on the highway. He was fined 1s.

Edwin John Clift, aged 19, from the High Street, serving with the Berkshire Regiment, died of wounds on 1 September 1918 near Mericourt-l'Abbe in France. He was probably wounded at Trones Wood during the Second Battle of the Somme. He was Arthur Kirby's cousin and had a brother and two half-brothers also serving in the army. On 8 October, William John Cook, aged 41, a cloth worker from the High Street, died of wounds near St Omer whilst serving with the King's Own Yorkshire Light Infantry. He left a wife and young daughter.

The influenza epidemic did not bypass Woodchester. The Medical Officer of Health, Dr Martin, ordered the school to be closed for three weeks from 14 October to 1 November inclusive. Perhaps this worked to some extent as the burial register does not show a significant increase in the number of deaths over the following months.

As the war drew to a close, Alfred Edward Dennis Palmer from Woodchester Mill Cottages, who had served in the Royal Navy on HMS *Iron Duke*, died from pneumonia on 4 November 1918 in hospital at South Queensferry. He is buried in St Mary's churchyard. His parents had already lost his younger brother, Leslie, aged 3, who had drowned in the mill pond of Woodchester Mill after disappearing from the bridge outside their house.

When the Armistice was signed at 11 a.m. on 11 November 1918, Woodchester's troubles were not over. Thomas Alfred Horwood, aged 22, of the Royal Garrison Artillery died of tuberculosis on the 18th of the month in a prisoner-of-war hospital (Lazarett zu Czersk) then in Prussia but now Poland.

His mother, a widow, lived in one of the almshouses at the top of Bospin Lane. Alfred was her last surviving child. After the war, the bodies of Commonweath servicemen in this area were moved to Poznan Old Garrison Cemetery.

Women of the village had played their parts in the war effort but have been very inadequately recorded. We know of several who worked in the munitions industry at Newman Hender in the valley or T.H. & J. Daniels in Stroud. Miss Eliza Workman was secretary of the Woodchester Vegetable Products Committee, collecting fresh fruit and vegetables, jam and preserves for the troops and the Fleet. The Allens and the Wises were active in the Red Cross.

War was not the only cause of devastation to Woodchester families who had already lost soldier sons. Two funerals were held at St Mary's church on Saturday, 11 January 1919. Evelyn May Wager (sister of Henry John), aged 21, and Maud Eliza Kirby (sister of Arthur), aged 18, both died from natural causes and were buried in the churchyard.

After the war, along with the rest of the country, Woodchester considered the erection of a suitable war memorial and a meeting was held in February 1919 to discuss the matter. The suggestions from the committee were for a Wayside Cross on land between North Woodchester and South Woodchester, facing the road leading to the station, on land which Mrs Bowles of Tower House had promised. There would also be a tablet in the church. However, the committee was not to have its way: the suggestion from the public was for a hall 'for the convenience of the young men of the neighbourhood' – no mention of the young women who had also played their part in the war effort! A vote was taken and the public hall was decided on with tablets in St Mary's and the Baptist church. The *Stroud Journal* reported that there was 'considerable disappointment amongst those who had favoured the Wayside Cross'. Nothing was said at the meeting about the Priory church, presumably the Wayside Cross erected in 1917 was considered a most suitable memorial.

Around the same time there was a proposal to provide village clubs under the sign of the Red Triangle (YMCA) as had existed for the use of soldiers in France and Flanders. Everything would appear to be fitting into place so far as Woodchester's memorials were concerned.

Soldiers were gradually returning home – in March, Sergeant Dick Turner of Home Farm arrived, according to the *Stroud Journal*, 'looking as fit as we have seen him, evidently the land of sun, sand and plagues [Egypt] agrees with him'. He had left his regiment in Aleppo on Army of Occupation duties. His brother, Frank, was already home from France. Gilbert Higgins of Lagger Lane, South Woodchester, was reported to be dangerously ill with appendicitis in Egypt. Fortunately, he appears to have had luck and the army medical services on his side as he survived.

By April, the war memorial subscriptions for tablets in church and chapel had been well supported and sufficient funds were in hand. There names of eighteen men who had lost their lives through the war were to be placed on both tablets. The proposed hall was to be called the 'Victory Club and Institute' and to be affiliated to the YMCA. Fundraising was still going on apace and various whist drives, concerts and dances were held throughout the year.

In June, a public meeting was held at the school to consider the format of Woodchester's peace celebrations. It was proposed to have a thanksgiving service with the rector, prior and nonconformist representative giving short addresses, followed by a sports tournament and dancing. Recognition was to be publicly given to all soldiers and sailors who 'wore His Majesty's uniform' and tokens in memory of the occasion were to be presented to the children.

Peace Day on 19 July in Woodchester was very busy. 'Church bells rang merry peals after which there was a general assembly in the Park field.' Marquees had been erected and preparations made for sports. However, all would not proceed smoothly. Church ministers made their addresses and medals (the gift of Mr Henry Workman) were presented to the children. A demonstration of maypole dancing took place but then 'rain commenced to fall heavily and the committee were perplexed as to the best course to pursue'. A few races were managed but in the end everyone adjourned to the marquee for tea, where the ex-soldiers of the parish were formed into a group and photographed. After tea, all outdoor activities were abandoned and 'the band [the Lightpill orchestra] and a number of young people repaired to the school, where dancing etc. occupied the remainder of the evening' (all quotations from the *Stroud Journal*).

The postponed sports took place on Saturday 10 August in the Park field and the weather was glorious! The maypole dancing, having been so well received on Peace Day, was repeated with King's Stanley brass band supplying the music. Enlarged portraits of a soldiers' group were presented to the men portrayed – this appears to be the photograph taken on Peace Day. There is a very touching sentence in the report of this occasion in the *Stroud Journal*: 'It is worthy of record that all discharged soldiers who won prizes handed them over to be sent to Charlie Boulton, a young discharged soldier who has been bedridden for many months owing to being "gassed" in France'.

On the following Wednesday, a 'dinner and smoking concert' was held at the Ram Inn Club Room in South Woodchester at the invitation of Mr and Mrs S. Birt, assisted by friends who subscribed. Before the dinner, the men and their friends were photographed; the group included Mr and Mrs Clement Allen of Southfields and the Revd G.E. Watton (Rector). Nearly ninety ex-servicemen with a few friends sat down to a 'substantial spread'. Lieutenant Wasley proposed the health of the returned soldiers, the rector read the list of the fallen and Mr Duke Laver of HM Navy thanked the host and hostess.

The photograph mentioned is believed to be the '1919 reunion' that has been frequently published. The presence of Mr and Mrs Allen in the front row suggests that they were probably the principal 'subscribers' and indeed Mrs Allen continued to host the annual event in memory of her husband. On the tenth anniversary, the men presented her with an album which was said to be one of her most treasured possessions.

Towards the end of the year, a discussion was held at Stroud Rural District Council about widening the High Street in South Woodchester from an average 12 feet 6 inches to 16 feet. The council agreed to pay £5 towards the alteration and to re-metal part of the road. At a time when a person could be fined 5*s* for riding a bicycle without lights or on the pavement, £5 may not have been seen as a very generous offer. As the parish was also concerned about the state of Atcombe Road, traffic problems are obviously not new.

As the calendar rolled over into 1920, Charles Frederick (Charlie) Boulton, aged 22, formerly of the Royal Garrison Artillery, died as a result of gas poisoning in the war and was buried in St Mary's churchyard on 10 January. He had been reported in the casualty list of 13 July 1917, a date which coincides with the introduction of mustard gas bombardments at Ypres. Having been discharged from the army on 15 March 1918 with a Silver War Badge, he had obviously been ill for some time. Thus Woodchester's roll of the fallen rose to nineteen and 'C.F. Boulton' was added at the bottom of the memorial plaques

The Ram Inn, South Woodchester, August 1919. (Bill Brunt collection)

The Piano Works in North Woodchester, showing the YMCA hut in the centre of the picture. (Bill Brunt collection)

in St Mary's and the Baptist chapel. Both these plaques are now in St Mary's following the closure of the Baptist chapel in 1981.

By this time, many villages in the Stroud area had already erected and unveiled memorials to their war dead. Woodchester seemed to be a bit slow but perhaps the reasons were around 'cutting our coat according to our cloth'!

A public meeting was called to consider whether the funds raised for a stone building to be called the Victory Hall should be applied to the 'fixing up' of a wooden hut provided free of cost by the YMCA. The meeting agreed that a stone building would be too expensive.

The Red Triangle Club (YMCA hut), the first in the Stroud valleys, was erected, largely by volunteer labour, on Selsley Road, by the then railway line. It consisted of several rooms and was obviously a substantial size. It was officially opened on Saturday, 25 September 1920 by Her Royal Highness Princess Marie Louise (granddaughter of Queen Victoria). Sadly, the hut was destroyed by fire during the Second World War.

The reports say that when the Princess left, she proceeded to a cenotaph erected in memory of the men of Woodchester who lost their lives, on which she placed a wreath. The cenotaph, an ionic cross made of Minchinhampton stone, at a cost of £180, was erected on land given by Captain and Mrs Bowles of Tower House, between the two parts, North and South, of the village.

This photograph is believed to be the opening of the Red Triangle (YMCA hut) in Selsley Road, North Woodchester. (Bill Brunt collection)

The money was raised from public subscriptions by a committee of the Anglican and Free Churches. This money may have been that raised for the Victory Hall which was not used.

At 3 p.m. on 31 October 1920, the Woodchester War Memorial was unveiled by William Dillon Ricketts, brother of George and his predecessor as headmaster of Woodchester School. The weather was, of course, inclement but despite this a large crowd assembled. The Stroud Military Band was in attendance. Prayers were led by the Revd R. Nott of Ebley (Congregational Minister). The Scripture reading was by the Revd W.J. Fox, pastor of the Baptist church. The Revd E.H. Hawkins (vicar of Holy Trinity, Stroud) read the solemn dedication and the rector, the Revd G.E. Watton, read the names inscribed. A two-minute silence was kept.

The names of nineteen men were carved in stone. The dates of their deaths range from 1914 to 1920 – killed in action, died of wounds, died or missing presumed dead. Of these, only three were laid to rest locally (one of whom was far from home) so the memorial would have been of some comfort to the families.

Although nineteen men are remembered, some with tenuous connections to the village, there are no women recorded. The name of Emma Josephine Rosamund Allen of Southfield House is certainly worthy of a mention here. Before the war, Emma and her sisters and mother were already active in the

Southfield House, home of the Allen family during the war. (Bill Brunt collection)

Gloucestershire Red Cross, Emma giving cookery demonstrations with Minnie Wise, then living at Oakley House. During the war, Emma became housekeeper at Standish VAD Hospital but had to retire when she could no longer continue through illness (appendicitis and pernicious anaemia). She was awarded a Silver War Badge (given to soldiers 'for services rendered' who were no longer able to serve), being only the second VA member in Gloucestershire to receive one. She died on 20 November 1917. The *Stroud News* reported: 'Of her it may be truly said that she died in the service of her country and so has made the supreme sacrifice as nobly as any who have fallen on the actual field of battle.'

Emma was buried in the family plot in St Mary's churchyard. Her memorial inscription is on the reverse of the base of the cross erected in memory of her brother Captain Clement Robert Wedgwood Allen of the Royal Welsh Regiment, who died when the rudder fell off his aeroplane and he crashed on Salisbury Plain in March 1914.

9
STONEHOUSE

STONEHOUSE HISTORY GROUP

EARLY DAYS OF THE WAR

In August 1914, men who were already soldiers, like Albert Baker of the Spa Inn, Oldends Lane, Stonehouse, had gone to fight in France. By September the government's recruitment drive was encouraging thousands more to join up. The *Stroud News* describes an enthusiastic scene in and around the Petty Sessional Court in High Street, Stonehouse, when twenty-seven young men stepped forward as volunteers.

The first mention of the war in Stonehouse Parish Council records came in the minutes of the Annual Meeting in March 1915. Those present stood in silence in memory of two dead soldiers, Private Baker and Rifleman Bullock. A book of condolence was prepared for their families.

Albert Baker. (Courtesy of the Baker family)

THE BAKER FAMILY

War memorials across the country are a reminder that the most devastating effect of war upon ordinary people was the loss of so many family members in tragic circumstances. The Baker family, who watched four precious sons go off to war, was typical of those families who suffered the loss of more than one person.

Eli and Elizabeth Baker married in 1886. In 1891 they were living at Downfield Terrace between Stroud and Cainscross. Eli was working as a hay trusser while Elizabeth cared for their two young sons, Albert, aged 3, and Frederick aged 2. By 1901 the family had moved to 16 Avenue Terrace in Stonehouse. Albert was working as a stable boy and groom while Frederick was a telegram messenger. Alexander, Reginald and Victoria had since been born and Cyril arrived a few years later.

In 1914 the family was running the Spa Inn in Oldends Lane. The men were occupied as hay trussers while the women and younger children helped run the pub. The family seemed healthy and happy living the country life. Their eldest son, Albert, had joined the army in 1906 as part of the Gloucestershire Regiment. In 1911 he was serving in Malta.

Albert Eli Baker

As a member of the Army Reserve, Albert Baker was one of the first to be mobilised for war in August 1914. His Brigade landed at Le Havre in France on 13 August and engaged in various actions on the Western Front. They were involved in the Battle of Mons and the subsequent retreat, the Battle of the Marne, the Battle of the Aisne and the First Battle of Ypres.

On 5 November 1914 at the Battle of Ypres, Albert became one of the first Stonehouse soldiers to be killed. His friend Albert Townsend, of Minchinhampton, wrote a moving letter to his mother which was reproduced in a local newspaper. The two Alberts had enjoyed a long friendship and Albert Baker was engaged to his friend's sister, Florence. The men were the same age and had enlisted in the Gloucestershire Regiment together. While in the army they had both been awarded bronze medallions by the Royal Life Saving Society for saving lives in India and Malta. Since leaving military service they had both been training to be railway signalmen, Baker at Ashby-de-la-Zouch and Townsend at Fishponds in Bristol. The two had travelled in the same brigade to France.

Private Baker was killed by a shell and Private Townsend wrote:

It was only my luck that I was not killed as well. I miss him every minute of the day. I wish it was me instead of him. I did the best I could for him. I buried him and it was the saddest thing I ever did. I have lost one of my truest friends and I cannot replace him.

Sadly, Lance-Corporal Albert Townsend was killed on 23 December 1914. Neither soldier has a marked grave. Albert Baker is recorded on the Menin Gate at Ypres and Albert Townsend on the Le Touret Memorial in France.

In his will Private Baker left £59 3s 11d to his father Eli Baker.

Alexander William Baker

The Bakers' third son, Alexander, was born in 1893. In 1911 he was living at the Spa Inn and working as a hay trusser for a hay merchant with his father and brothers. In June 1914 he married Lottie Vick. As a married man he may have been excused from joining up immediately, however, he became a gunner in the Royal Garrison Artillery (RGA). He was in the 129th Heavy Battery and probably went to France in 1916. Heavy Batteries RGA were equipped with heavy guns, sending large-calibre high-explosive shells in fairly flat trajectory fire. As British artillery tactics developed, the Heavy Batteries were most often employed in destroying or neutralising the enemy artillery, as well as putting destructive fire down on strongpoints, dumps, stores, roads and railways behind enemy lines. The men were shelled and gassed by the enemy.

Alexander survived until the Armistice but was unlucky enough to die from the effects of gas on 12 November 1918. His great niece, Helen Bell, was told

Alexander William Baker.
(Courtesy of the Baker family)

that the family were so traumatised by the loss of two sons that their names were rarely mentioned and it seemed that they scarcely visited Alexander's widow Lottie. She never remarried and died in 1966.

Reginald Walter Baker

Reginald was born on 15 August 1896. By 1901 the family had moved to Avenue Terrace and he attended Eastington Primary School. He later followed the rest of his family into the haymaking business.

He was a member of the Gloucestershire Yeomanry which divided into separate units during the war. He was in the 1st Royal Gloucestershire Hussars who fought in Egypt and at Gallipoli. As part of the cavalry, he took part in the battles in the Middle East. He became a signaller and also fought in Mesopotamia (Iraq) and India. His brigade was transferred to many different locations as the war progressed and on 15 April 1917 he was lucky to escape with his life when the ship he was travelling on, the *Cameronia*, was torpedoed by the German submarine *U33* en route from Marseilles to Alexandria, Egypt, 150 nautical miles from Malta while carrying 2,650 troops. The *Cameronia* sank in forty minutes, resulting in 210 deaths. Some of the survivors were picked up by the escorting destroyer, HMS *Rifleman*. As the U-boat was still in the area, the remaining survivors had to be picked up the next morning by a sloop from Malta.

Writing to his parents, Reg said:

> … just a line to let you know I am saved and un-wounded. I expect you see by the papers that the 'Cameronia' was torpedoed in the Mediterranean. Talk about a panic, I have been in a fix before now but never one like this. We got hit 5.30 Sunday night and in 35 minutes the boat was out of sight. I was one of the lifeboat crew, but we did not stand a rat's chance, as the fellows were mad and before we could get the boat off the pulleys she was packed with men.
>
> The only thing I worry about is my pal, I believe he has gone under, but of course I cannot say for certain as there were heaps of fellows in the water when our destroyer came away.
>
> Of course one is bound to feel the shock. Some of the poor boys were knocked out before they touched the water, and a lot got knocked out by the lifeboats capsizing, but I cannot tell you how many have been put out as I do not know. I am living in hope that there are not many. I have lost everything except what I stand up in, but expect to be issued with some more in a day's time.
>
> Remember me to all at home and tell them I am still alive and kicking.

On 11 May 1917 the *Stroud News* reported Lance-Corporal R. W. Baker's rescue from the *Cameronia*, in which he praised the fine rescue work of the crew of the British destroyer:

> I owe my life to a Jack Tar. If it had not been for him I should have been under the destroyer. He flung a piece of rope to me and pulled me in … I think we ought to be proud of the Navy … The Captain of the destroyer deserves the DSO. He would not leave until nearly every available man was picked up.

Reginald survived the war and returned to his family. In 1923 he married Hilda Shakespeare and they had two sons and a daughter. He set up a successful haulage business in Stonehouse – R. W. Baker & Sons – which was carried on by his son. He died in 1974.

Reginald Baker was in the Gloucestershire Yeomanry (Royal Gloucester Hussars). (Courtesy of the Baker family)

Frederick Baker

Frederick was gassed during the war. He survived but remained in poor health. He took over the Spa Inn from his parents and ran it from 1931 to 1950.

After the War

Like so many others of that generation, the lives of the Baker family were changed forever. It is said that the parents never recovered from the loss of their two sons. Lottie Baker lost her husband after only a few years during which he was away at the front. Victoria May and Cyril were young enough to rebuild their lives, get married and have children. Reginald's daughter Pamela Bird and granddaughter Helen Bell and Cyril's son Bruce contributed memories and photos to this chapter.

BENJAMIN DOOLEY PARKIN

If there can be said to be a positive outcome to the First World War, it may be that some of those who survived the horrors of the war came back determined to improve the lives of ordinary people.

Born on 2 July 1879 in the village of Riddings near Alfreton in Derbyshire, Benjamin Parkin was the son of Samuel Parkin, a colliery clerk. His mother Elizabeth gave her maiden name, Dooley, to her son as a second name. His grandfathers and uncles had all been mine workers but his father, Samuel, a younger son, was of a more academic bent. In 1861 he was a pupil teacher and in 1871 a clerk. It is likely that he encouraged his eldest son, Benjamin, to get an education.

Benjamin qualified as a certificated teacher at St John's College, Battersea. In September 1906 he was appointed headmaster of Winterbourne Down All Saints' School in Bristol.

In 1911 the headmaster of Stonehouse Council School, Mr John Westacott, retired. Benjamin Parkin, then aged 32, applied for the job and was successful. He and his family moved to Stonehouse and he commenced his duties on 18 October 1911.

Benjamin had first served in the army while he was a young teacher, as a volunteer in the 2nd South Middlesex Volunteer regiment at the turn of the twentieth century, soon after the start of the Boer War. He was promoted to sergeant and was one of the bodyguards to Queen Victoria when she laid the foundation stone of the South Kensington Museum. When the First World War began in 1914, he volunteered for the army again. Initially he was rejected on medical grounds. There had been scarlet fever in the school in 1914 and he had been off sick for seven weeks. Also his sight was poor, which may have been a factor. However, as more soldiers died in the fighting, regulations were relaxed and he was accepted into his old territorial battalion in June 1916.

Parkin did his initial training and became a lance-corporal. Those in charge spotted his potential and he was sent on a number of courses where he easily topped the list of NCOs. After having said a sad farewell to his family, on the eve of departure to France he was withdrawn and sent for Officer training. This meant he stayed in England until August 1917. At the end of his training he was again top of his class and selected to sit next to the colonel at the final dinner. On 28 August he joined the 7th West Riding Regiment and set off for France on 4 November 1917.

Parkin described the class system that existed in the army. As a young officer he had a servant who stayed with him throughout the war. However, he emphasised that there was a great spirit of togetherness, 'officers and men are comrades'. He describes his Commanding Officer's speech before heading into battle as 'reminiscent of *Henry V*'. The CO was 25 years old and was killed a fortnight later from a direct hit by a shell. Later, Parkin describes how devastated the men were when the Brigadier was killed, 'we loved him'.

Parkin suffered terrible conditions in the trenches, as did all the men, but never had to go 'over the top' into battle. Because he was a good map reader and an intelligent man, he was appointed as an intelligence officer. This meant

he had to receive messages from aeroplanes and get them to the officer in charge. This often involved running along the trenches from shell hole to shell hole under bombardment but, even though men were killed either side of him, Parkin was never wounded. Many of his friends were killed at the Battle of Bourlon Wood. Travelling on a train across France, the train was bombed and machine-gunned but, miraculously, Parkin remained physically unscathed.

The first time he heard enemy shelling he was terrified. He wanted to find a hole and hide in it. But as time went

Benjamin Dooley Parkin. (© Pip Parkin)

on he became used to it and would stand at the edge of the trench and watch the artillery with pride. Most of the time the men were waiting for orders to attack. They were filled with apprehension waiting for the battles at Arras and Vimy Ridge.

Benjamin was promoted to captain, a rank he was proud of for the rest of his life. At the end of the war he became an education officer with the army on the Rhine Adult Education Scheme, designed to prepare troops for civilian life. When his division returned to England he was given a similar post with the 51st Highland Division.

Twelve years after the war, Benjamin wrote a diary of his wartime experiences. This was deposited in the Imperial War Museum and Stonehouse History Group has a copy.

After the war Captain Parkin returned to the Council School on 1 July 1919, where he remained as headmaster until he retired in 1939. He was one of the most influential men in Stonehouse during the first half of the twentieth century: chairman of the Parish Council, Chief ARP Warden for the Stroud area during the Second World War, as well as president of the Stonehouse Branch of the British Legion and a Justice of the Peace.

Benjamin Dooley Parkin died, aged 82, on 10 January 1962. He left an impressive legacy of service to his town and country.

Captain Parkin, representing the British Legion in Belgium, is seen here laying a wreath at one of the many memorial services held across Europe after the First World War. (© Pip Parkin)

STANDISH HOSPITAL

The King family had rented Standish House from 1884 to 1897, when they moved to Newark Park. Before the war, Mary King, the eldest daughter of the family, was involved in organising a Red Cross Nursing Association and the training of Red Cross nurses. She realised that, in the event of a European war, there would be a need for hospitals to cope with those wounded. During 1914, while it was empty, Mary approached its owner, Lord Sherborne. He agreed to loan Standish House for use as a hospital and to have it decorated, fitted with electric lights, additional baths and toilet facilities.

The *Stroud News* reported that local people were invited to look round the hospital on Easter Monday 1915 and more than 700 people visited that day. They were asked for gifts to assist in the running of the hospital. When the hospital opened on 13 May there were 100 beds and eight fully trained staff, plus local volunteers from the Red Cross in Stonehouse and surrounding areas. Many had been trained by Mary King herself, who was the commandant.

All of the wounded soldiers came from the Beaufort War Hospital in Bristol. The staff had only two hours' notice before the first patients arrived. There were thirty-one in the first batch, of which fourteen were stretcher cases. Although it was May, snow was falling and it was very cold, so the gardeners had to light the fires throughout the new hospital. It was early closing day for shops in Stonehouse but local people rallied round to collect food from their homes to feed the soldiers. Local people also transported the wounded soldiers from the railway station.

Shortly after the hospital opened, two wooden huts (known as 'The Chalets') were built on the grounds. They housed a further thirty beds to accommodate more wounded. Those soldiers who were able to get out of bed were expected to wear their uniforms and to help other soldiers who could not dress or wash themselves. Those who were well enough were allowed to go

Miss Mary King, OBE
Commandant

Mary King stayed in the former butler's room throughout the war and did not join her family at Newark Park until the hospital closed in early 1919. During the war, some of the wounded convalesced at Newark Park to free up beds for those with more serious injuries. Mary was awarded the OBE for her efforts during the war. (Courtesy of the Stonehouse History Group (SHG) collection)

Soldiers in front of Standish Hospital. (Wilf Merrett collection, Museum in the Park, Stroud)

Hospital staff in November 1917. (SHG collection)

into Stonehouse during the day. Some even caught the train to Stroud but they had to be back by 6.30 p.m. or they had no supper! They made lots of friends in the village and sometimes went to the cinema (believed to be the Star Cinema & Theatre at Lansdown in Stroud).

Hospital staff

Work on the land and in the factories was unacceptable for women from better off families, but they could help the national war effort by caring for wounded soldiers. Such women joined organisations like the Red Cross and the Voluntary Aid Detachments (VADs). Standish Hospital had mainly voluntary, unmarried, female Red Cross and VAD staff plus eight professional nursing sisters and several medical staff (only one was resident).

There were more than seventy volunteers, most of them part-time. The full-time staff lived in the attic accommodation and in the lodge. Between shifts, most of the volunteers cycled or walked between home and the hospital. A total of 2,292 sick and wounded soldiers were treated at the hospital by local Red Cross and VAD volunteers.

Duties of VAD volunteers included:

- looking after the soldiers
- scrubbing the floors
- working as scullery maids
- working in the laundry
- stoking the fires
- laying the tables
- darning socks in spare time!

These women from well-off families suddenly had wounded soldiers depending on them. Like many tasks in this war, women had to take over from men who had gone to the Forces. They found they were capable of doing men's work and being independent – and liked it!

The nurses became very fond of the soldiers and often brought them extra cigarettes and sweets. In turn, the soldiers put on plays and even taught the nurses how to shoot a gun. Stonehouse had been a quiet village before the war and local people must have found it strange to have a lot of soldiers coming down from Standish every day, in a variety of uniforms, while their own men were away fighting. It must have brought home to the locals how dangerous it was to be a fighting soldier – particularly since the Standish patients would have had first-hand experience.

FIRST SUCCESSFUL LANDING OF AN AEROPLANE IN STONEHOUSE

On 9 August 1916, an aeroplane landed in the field between Bridgend and the railway viaduct at Beard's Mill. Captain Eric Dixon of the Royal Flying Corps had been given permission to see his brother Hugh before he left for service in France. The *Stroud News* reported that Captain Dixon landed within 100 yards of his home (Downton House, Stanley Downton) and that hundreds of people came to see the plane – and awaited his departure at 6 p.m. There was loud cheering, waving of handkerchiefs and hats when he took off. Captain Dixon circled the area, waved to the crowd and soon disappeared from sight. Two little girls, Marjorie and Doris Flint from Stanley Downton, took a collection on behalf of Standish Hospital. Sadly, following a serious flying accident on 17 August 1917, Captain Dixon died of his injuries. He was 27 years old and had been married for just nine months.

WYCLIFFE COLLEGE

In April 1917 the school's magazine, *Wycliffe Star*, reported that nearly a hundred of the boys had gardens or potato plots which, the *Star* noted, had become a 'national craze'. The whole field on the north side of the Midland Railway Branch Line had been dug over. In his speech at prize-giving the headmaster commented: 'Whatever Wycliffe is likely to lack in the coming twelve months, it certainly will not be potatoes!'

During the summers of 1916 to 1918, aid was provided to local farmers. The usual hours worked by the boys were 11 a.m. until 7 p.m. or 2 p.m. until 8 p.m. Those starting at 11 a.m. took their own rations for lunch but farmers were expected to supply tea. All proceeds went to wartime charities.

In the summer of 1918 the *Star* observed that 'by far the greatest harvest modern England ever knew' was ripening in the fields – but the labourers were many thousands fewer than in previous years. The Ministry of National Service gathered volunteers of every sort and appealed for help from the schools throughout the country. Wycliffe provided a party of fifty who were sent to Chitterne on the Wiltshire Downs, where there were 3,000 acres of corn. When the party arrived the binding machines were just beginning their work and, for the next twenty-four days, the party's main role was to gather up and stook the sheaves. The party worked a total of 6,017 hours for which they were paid a total of £100 5s 8d (approximately £5,900 in today's money). This, together with the regulation Treasury grant of about 18s a boy, enabled the party to meet all expenses. The government also provided third-class railway tickets and tickets for cycles to be carried on trains. When the party left they had 'seen the harvest home' on four farms.

Serving their country

When the war broke out almost half of the former pupils who had left Wycliffe in the previous thirty years joined the Armed Forces. By the end of the war around 550 Old Wycliffians had served. Of those, seventy-seven had died. Six DSOs, thirty-seven Military Crosses, four Distinguished Flying Crosses, seventeen other military awards and thirty-six 'mentions in despatches' had been awarded.

Second Lieutenant T.M. Sibly, a teacher at Wycliffe, was mentioned in despatches for his service in France and the Balkans.

The death of former pupil Rex Bird at the Somme in 1916 was a great blow to all who knew him. He had led an exemplary life, being successful in academic work and on the sports field, while also setting an example of gentlemanliness and kindness to all.

Wycliffe chapel clock tower and spire

After the war it was agreed to commemorate the men who died by building a clock tower and spire on to the chapel. The new clock tower and spire were dedicated in July 1921, rebuilt during the 1950s after a fire in 1939 and restored in 2012. A plaque inside the chapel giving the names of the dead reads:

> The tower of this chapel is dedicated to the memory of the old boys of Wycliffe College who gave their lives for England in the Great War 1914–1918.
> Greater love hath no man than this that a man lay down his life for his friends.
> These served and died in the deathless cause of right and liberty. Their names are written in the book of life and are engraven here that we who read with what a great price freedom still is bought, may pay our tribute of reverence, gratitude and affection, and give all praise to God.

WOMEN OF STONEHOUSE

Since so many men went off to war there was an urgent need to fill their former jobs. In 1917, for example, Vowles' brushworks in Stonehouse reported that between seventy and eighty employees were serving in the Armed Forces. So, for the first time, women were employed in jobs traditionally done by men.

Before the war Jessie Louisa Durham worked as a dressmaker. In 1914 she became one of the women who delivered the mail around Stonehouse. Because of a shortage of staff, the Post Office had to reduce deliveries to twice daily.

Quedgeley Munitions Factory opened in March 1916. By June there were 2,420 workers – 2,113 of them women. When TNT poisoning was identified as a hazard, the numbers dropped. After a newspaper appeal, the workforce rose to 6,364 in March 1917. Pay was £1 for a 48-hour week. A railway station was built at the factory so that workers from Stonehouse and Stroud could get to work easily.

Miss Kathleen May Jenner Davies, of Hayward's End, Stonehouse, served as an ambulance driver in Serbia and France. She was awarded the Samaritan Cross by the Crown Prince of Serbia in 1918. After the war, she compiled (under her married name, Lady Kathleen Fetherston-Godley) a Remembrance book of the fallen soldiers with their photos – *Lest We Forget: World War 1, 1914–1918 Book of Remembrance*, which was presented to the Royal British Legion Stonehouse Branch in 1921.

THE AFTERMATH

On 17 November 1918, social reformer Beatrice Webb, who was born and brought up in Standish House, wrote: 'Every day one meets saddened women,

Female workers at Lister's in Dursley. (Courtesy of the Baker family)

Miss Kathleen May Jenner Davies. (Courtesy of Howard Beard)

with haggard faces and lethargic movements, and one dare not ask after husband or son.' As in other communities throughout the country, there was much grief and many broken men in Stonehouse.

The *Stroud News* recorded the names of 176 Stonehouse men who served in the Armed Forces, eight who gained distinctions such as the Military Medal, and fifty-two who were killed in action, died of their wounds, or were missing. These figures do not represent all who served, as men who joined up after 1915, and survived, are not included.

Sergeant Major Charles Henry Gardner, 11th Hussars, of Stonehouse had been awarded the French Medaille Militaire for gallantry (during operations between 21 and 30 August 1914) and had been wounded. He was also 'mentioned in despatches' and awarded the Good Conduct and Long Service Medals. In 1919, after twenty-three years' service, he was a chronic rheumatic, 'no longer physically fit for war service', and unemployed.

WAR MEMORIALS

The war ended in 1918 at 'the 11th hour of the 11th day of the 11th month'. A War Memorial was erected on the Town Green. St Cyr's church records state: 'Memorial to Stonehouse men who fell in the Great War, unveiled by Miss Emily Davies and dedicated by the Rev. R. P. Waugh, Vicar, August 12, 1919.' The War Memorial is still a focal point for the community. It was beautifully restored in 2009 and remains the meeting place for the annual Remembrance Service.

At a Parish Council meeting in June 1919, the chairman, John Westacott, remarked that he thought a recreation ground would provide a suitable Peace Memorial. That was strongly supported by the other councillors. Within six months Mr J.C.C. Kimmins had acquired the land near Laburnum Walk and offered it to the parish. In 1920, the Comrades of the Great War contributed £40 for the recreation ground and Mr A.S. Winterbotham of Stonehouse Court gave £100. The Laburnum memorial ground has been well-used by the community ever since. In 2014 new play equipment and a boules court were installed. Community events are held there and it is a quiet peaceful place, with beautiful views to the Cotswold Escarpment.

10

BRIMSCOMBE

THE COLE FAMILY'S EXPERIENCE

TINA BLACKMAN

Mr and Mrs W.H. Cole lived at Bourne House, Brimscombe, with their seven children – four boys and three girls – and a number of household staff. William Henry Cole JP was a prominent figure in both public and business life. As well as being part owner and director of Cole and Lewis, a large bacon factory in Cirencester, he held senior roles in several other organisations including the Cirencester Urban District Council and the Cirencester Gas Company. He had been appointed Justice of the Peace for Gloucestershire in 1895, sitting regularly on the Cirencester Bench. The family belonged to the Anglican church and Mr Cole was Worshipful Master of the Cotteswold Lodge of Freemasons.

At the outbreak of the Great War, the three eldest Cole sons, Fritz, Cyril and Clifford, immediately signed up to join the war effort. Fritz (23) worked in the family business and was also a Territorial, being a second lieutenant in the 5th Gloucestershire Regiment. Cyril (21) was academically inclined and, as a graduate from the Engineering Faculty of Glasgow University with a Bachelor of Science degree, had started an apprenticeship at the Fairfield Shipbuilding Yards in Glasgow. Clifford (18) had recently graduated from Marlborough College, Wiltshire, and Maxwell (16) was still boarding at Marlborough College as his older brothers had before him.

Fritz, as an existing member of the 5th Territorial Battalion, was immediately sent to Chelmsford, in Essex, for training. There was a huge influx of volunteers wanting to join the 5th Gloucestershire Regiment and it had to be divided into two groups, known as the 1/5th and 2/5th. Fritz was part of the 1/5th Gloucestershire Regiment and was soon promoted to Captain. The 1/5th Battalion, Gloucestershire Regiment, was part of the 145th Brigade, 48th (South Midland) Division. Their final training was undertaken far from home in Danbury, near Chelmsford.

Cyril and Clifford signed up to the 2/5th Gloucestershire Regiment and were sent to Northampton and Chelmsford for military training. They were soon promoted to officers.

In March 1915, Fritz was the first brother to sail to France on the RMS *Invicta* with his battalion. After a long march in the bitterly cold northerly wind and some distance in cattle trucks the men were assigned to the Ploegsteert Wood Sector in Belgium. Fritz wrote daily to his sweetheart, Miss M.R. Davies. They missed each other dreadfully and, as the letters were censored, they were limited as to what could be shared. Rosamund, as she was known, lived at Fretherne Lodge in the settlement of Fretherne with her parents the Revd C.D.P. and Mrs J. Davies.

By July 1915, Fritz was acting commanding officer of D Company in the trenches at Hébuterne. Leave was rare but in April 1916 Fritz was able to return to England for a short time. He and Rosamund became engaged, but did not set a date as they didn't want a 'war wedding'. Many people still thought the war wasn't going to last much longer. Fritz was disappointed to be called back to the front two days earlier than expected. On his return, he was given the news that he was now permanently in the role of commanding officer of D Company.

A month later, in May 1916, Cyril and Clifford and the rest of the 2/5th Gloucestershire Regiment arrived in France. Clifford sailed on *HMT 861* with thirty officers and other ranks and Cyril, as part of the Transport Division,

Clifford Cole. (Courtesy of Marlborough College)

travelled on the SS *Inventor* with the Brigade Headquarters. By June they had travelled to Laventie, where the men prepared to enter the trenches for the first time. Three of the four Cole brothers were now in France.

On 15 June 1916 the 2/5th Gloucestershire Battalion had their first experience of trench duty in the Fauquissart-Laventie sector. It was an eventful first week. On 18 June, Lieutenant Clifford Cole was promoted to captain. The very next day, he was the first officer from the battalion to lose his life when he was killed by an aerial torpedo. In his book *2/5th Battalion Gloucestershire Regiment 1914–1918*, A.F. Barnes (MC) relates:

> He had been with [the Battalion] since its early days and by his efficiency and good nature he had won the esteem of both officers and men. His death, taking place so soon after the Battalion had gone to France, came as a blow.

A dreadful week followed for the battalion. Four hundred and sixty-three soldiers lie today at the Royal Irish Rifles graveyard in Laventie. Six 2nd/5th Gloucestershire graves lie side-by-side in row II.J:

Pte J. Hall, II.J.1, 21 June 16, Age 22
Pte C.W. Jackson, II.J.2, 21 June 16, Age 19
Pte F. Yeldham, II.J.3, 21 June 16, Age 39
Pte E. Skellern, II.J.4, 20 June 16, Age 20
Lt C. Cole, II.J.5, 19 June 16, Age 20
Pte W. Phipps, II.J.6, 20 June 16, Age unknown

July 1916 is etched in history as the beginning of the Battle of the Somme. The 1/5th Gloucesters were heavily involved in the attack on Ovillers. On 23 July, 145b Infantry Brigade (including 1/5th Gloucesters) was ordered to attack. One officer died and seven others, including Fritz Cole, were wounded. A telegram was delivered to the Cole family home in Brimscombe which read:

> T/4551 regret to inform you Capt. FW Cole 5th Glosters Regt admitted one Red Cross Hospital. Le Touquet 24th July gunshot wound elbow.

Fritz was immediately sent back to England to recover. In September, Fritz and Rosamund were married at Fretherne. Once married, Fritz and Rosamund moved to a small flat in the city of Bath near where Fritz had been sent to train officers at Prior Park. Although he was considered medically unfit to return to the front, family history relates that this may have been due to being badly gassed in the trenches rather than the wound to his elbow referred to in the telegram.

While Fritz was on the Somme, and Cyril was further north, their youngest brother, Maxwell Gerard Cole, was about to graduate from Marlborough College where he had been part of their Officers Training Corps. The college records show that in February 1916 he was promoted to corporal, and further promoted in May 1916 to sergeant. Maxwell's application to the army for an Appointment to the Special Reserve of Officers shows he had experience on a motorcycle and had at some point broken his arm playing rugby football. His photo shows him as being of slight build and his records show he was 5ft 11in tall and weighed 142lb. He was granted Second Lieutenant Land Forces in August 1916 and accepted to the General List and Christ Church College for instruction in aviation. Maxwell spent time in Croydon, Surrey, during his training with No. 17 Reserve Squadron. Training was in two-seater aeroplanes, each plane carrying a pilot and an observer who took photographs. He graduated with his Pilot's Certificate in December 1916. In early 1917 Maxwell was attached to No. 1 Squadron of the Royal Flying Corps at Bailleul, France. No. 1 Squadron was one of the first fighter squadrons. Pilots who were transferred during this time had never flown single-seater planes before and accidents were commonplace. On 5 February, two days after arrival, Maxwell crashed his first plane, a Nieuport 17 with serial number A6618. It was wrecked during landing and initially written off. However, after being returned to the depot it was decided to reconstruct it.

The Battle of Arras raged throughout April 1917. The death toll for pilots was terrible and the month became known as Bloody April. No. 1 Squadron was not hit as badly as some other squadrons. Although parachutes were used by observers in kite balloons, they were not issued to pilots. It has been estimated that one third of lives lost at the front in planes could have been saved by the use of parachutes. On 18 May, No. 1 Squadron was ordered by the Wing to carry out a risky attack on German balloons. The squadron's commanding officer, G.C. St P. de Dombasle, was not happy but was required to follow orders. A group of six pilots headed out in the evening in single-seater Nieuport 17s and 23s. Two balloons were destroyed with their German observers jumping clear. Only three of the pilots returned to the squadron with one of them being seriously injured. One pilot, T.H. Lines, was taken prisoner and two pilots were killed by anti-aircraft artillery. One of these was a Canadian, Second Lieutenant Lindsay Drummond. The other was 18-year-old Maxwell Cole, whose plane went down in flames.

Back in England Rosamund was having a difficult pregnancy. Fritz was working long days training officers at Prior Park so Rosamund moved back to her parents at Fretherne, as she had been instructed by the doctor to rest. After a difficult labour, baby Michael William Cole was born on 10 June 1917. Maxwell was to have been his godfather. Rosamund's brother, Home, sent a telegram. 'Best of future luck for you and your son. May he never have to go to war.'

At this time Cyril Cole was still part of the 2/5th Gloucesters, who formed part of the 184th Brigade, 61st (2/South Midland) Division, XI Corps, First Army. They were then transferred to Arras, XIX Corps, Fifth Army and their next major action was at the Third Battle of Ypres, also known as the Battle of Passchendaele. On 22 August, 2/5th Battalion was involved in fierce fighting to take the concrete fortification at Pond Farm. On that day alone, three officers and sixteen other ranks were killed, one Officer and fifty-one other ranks wounded and one other rank missing from the 2/5th Gloucestershire Regiment. Passchendaele was very costly in human terms. Over 300,000 Allied and 200,000 German soldiers lost their lives in the fighting and endless rain led to the offensive being known as the 'Battle of Mud'. By then the USA had joined the war in support of the Allies.

On 19 May 1917, Max had been officially listed as Missing in Action. A short time later the Germans dropped a message stating that Second Lieutenant T.H. Lines had been taken prisoner and Second Lieutenants M.G. Cole and L. Drummond had been killed. On 19 June 1917, Max's army file states that a German newspaper, *Norddeutsche Allgemeine Zeitung*, had reported him as being killed and surmised that this information was probably correct. On 10 August 1917 a letter officially confirming Max's death was sent to his father at Bourne House. The letter told of the message dropped by the Germans and explained that such messages were usually reliable. The letter was typewritten but a note is handwritten at the bottom stating, 'No reference to the dropped message should be made in any public announcement.' Max was buried in Houthem Military Cemetery by the Germans.

Maxwell Cole. (Courtesy of Marlborough College)

Cyril Cole remained at the front. The 2/5th Gloucesters' final battle was experienced during the Battle of Valenciennes in the area of Maresches and St Hubert in the first week of November. The hold on Maresches was maintained and on 2 November three German officers and 240 other ranks were taken prisoner. Also captured were German weapons including twenty-one machine guns. The 2/5th were relieved by the 13th Battalion Middlesex Regiment at 7 p.m. and they arrived at their billets for the night at 9 p.m.

On 11 November 1918 the Armistice was signed and the First World War came to an end. Cyril Cole and Elsie Kathleen Williams-White were married a few weeks later. Cyril then returned to France to help with demobilisation. Unfortunately, an influenza epidemic swept the world at this time. By May 1919 it had killed 20 million people – many more than the 8 million killed by the war. For unknown reasons it affected young, healthy people more than children or the elderly. Tragically, one of these was Cyril, who died of bronchial pneumonia in March 1919.

In June 1919 Fritz was awarded an MBE. He returned to the family business after the war but the Great Depression meant that business held more challenges than before. Fritz, Rosamund, son Michael and daughter Penelope (born in April 1920) moved to Benson, Oxfordshire, chosen because it was halfway between the business premises in Cirencester and the customers in London. Fritz became a popular man in the village of Benson and the wider neighbourhood.

Mr William Henry Cole and Mrs Catherine Martha Cole remained in Brimscombe until they died in 1932. Although William retained his trade connection, he was forced to retire from his many commitments due to ill health, including crippling arthritis. Mrs Cole is reported as having been an invalid for a long time before her death. The elder members of the family relate that she was never the same after losing her sons.

Cyril Cole. (Courtesy of Marlborough College)

During the Second World War Fritz Cole led the Special Constabulary in Oxfordshire and for many years he was a committed Freemason and the churchwarden of St Helen's church, Benson. As the sole surviving Cole brother, he died prematurely in 1955 and his son Michael believed this may have been as a result of his time in the trenches. Michael Cole said that for many of those soldiers, health problems showed themselves years later. Fritz Cole is buried in the churchyard at St Helen's church, Benson.

Cyril, Clifford and Maxwell lie in the carefully tended cemeteries of the Commonwealth War Graves Commission. Cyril lies in Etaples Military Cemetery, France. There is a message on the grave from his young wife. Max was originally buried in Houthem Military Cemetery by the German Army. He was reinterred by the Commonwealth to Oosttaverne Wood Cemetery, Belgium after the war. Clifford lies in the small and peaceful Royal Irish Rifles graveyard in Laventie.

After the death of Michael William Cole in 2009, Tina Blackman researched, wrote and published *The Three Uncles: The Cole Brothers in the Great War* so that the Cole brothers and in particular Fritz William Cole – her great-grandfather – would not be forgotten.

11

AFTERWORD

AFTERWARDS

PETER EVANS

This picture shows Brimscombe at peace, just before the Great War. Our village school and church are in the top left corner of the photograph. Jubilee field, below the terrace, was the only almost level public recreation space amid the hills.

I was born in a house at the end of the dark-bricked Victoria Terrace on 22 March 1932, where my father was born too.

I gradually became aware of the devastation and horror of the war that nobody in this village much talked about. It was still numbed from the conflict. The young Brimscombe men killed in it, never out of mind, were remembered particularly on each Armistice anniversary by the bereaved, their heads bowed at the war memorial among British Legion flags. Those young men did not grow old as we that were left have. I was moved as a child, and always am, by the sound in the silence of the Last Post and Reveille.

Brimscombe, Britain and Europe would never be the same again. In the Foreign Office on 3 August 1914, Sir Edward Grey, Foreign Secretary, looked out of the window into the sunset across St James's Park in London as the lights came on along the Mall. He said to a friend, 'The lamps are going out all over Europe.' His words have been much remembered, later inspiring the Second World War song, 'When The Lights Go On Again.' We lost so much, and not only the dead.

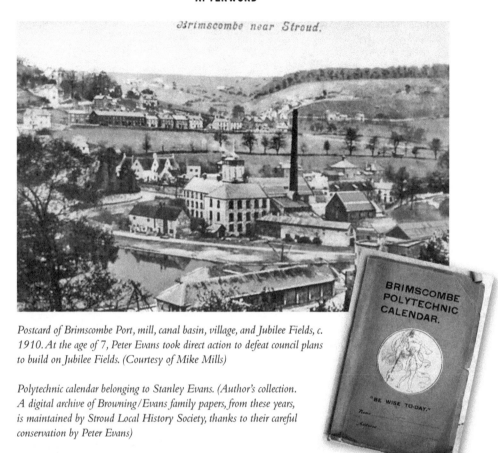

Brimscombe near Stroud.

Postcard of Brimscombe Port, mill, canal basin, village, and Jubilee Fields, c. 1910. At the age of 7, Peter Evans took direct action to defeat council plans to build on Jubilee Fields. (Courtesy of Mike Mills)

Polytechnic calendar belonging to Stanley Evans. (Author's collection. A digital archive of Browning/Evans family papers, from these years, is maintained by Stroud Local History Society, thanks to their careful conservation by Peter Evans)

Brimscombe was a settled place before 1914, looking to the future. I have my father's schoolbook, in his own hand, from Brimscombe Polytechnic in 1909, giving a vivid picture of life there and in the village. He has drawn the first aeroplane and says he has made a model.

The Poly's foundation was inspired by the owner of one of the prosperous local mills. It produced a calendar and students' diary for the school year 1913–14, a remarkable record of further education then in this village for boys and girls after they left Brimscombe junior school and others nearby. Photographs show the old headquarters of the Canal Company in which it was housed. In the commercial class, each smartly dressed pupil is working at a typewriter. The Polytechnic developed later into a craft school and the Central School at Downfield, now part of Marling School.

The training was for work. My father went on to become an apprentice at Abdela & Mitchell, the boat builders next to the canal, which exported to distant parts of the world. Both my grandfathers worked there, Grampy Evans, the foreman, Grampy Browning, my mother's father, and his two sons, Percy

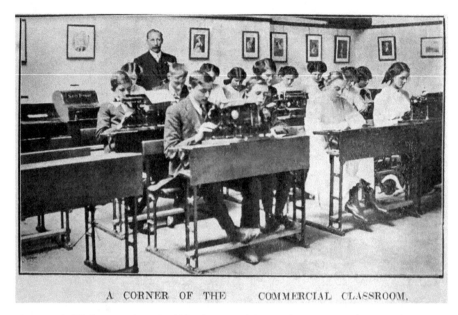

A CORNER OF THE COMMERCIAL CLASSROOM.

Commercial skills being taught at the old headquarters of the Canal Company. Each smartly dressed student is working at a typewriter. (Author's collection)

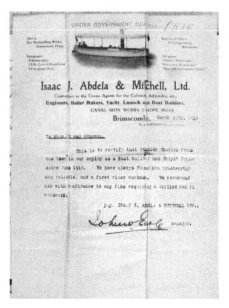

Abdela & Mitchell Ltd letterhead.
(Author's collection)

Violet Browning wearing a fine hat.
(Author's collection)

and Claude. Claude trained on the engineering side and went on to work under Frank Whittle on his engine for the first jet aircraft to fly.

The village seemed secure, with a flourishing church on the hill, two chapels, its own fire engine, brewery, one-time bank, public houses, football team, mills and shops to make it self-sufficient. For a treat, my father went to the coffee tavern near Brimscombe corner for a meal of faggots, which was then the local gourmet choice. Trains went to London, and locally a railcar to Gloucester stopped at stations and halts on the line. Passengers were welcomed aboard the railcar by Mr Furley, the conductor and guard, who always wore a splendid flower in his buttonhole and worshipped at the Wesleyan chapel.

Buses groaned up the hills to surrounding villages. Farmers, butchers and bakers fed everyone. A death would be marked by the tolling of the Brimscombe church bell, once for every year of the age of the departed. The village would count the number and curtains would be drawn in respect.

But then came the war. My mother, Violet Browning before marriage, recalls what happened in a recorded interview with her – a heartfelt account of life before, during and after 1914–18. She lived in Minchinhampton, but reactions in Brimscombe and elsewhere would have been much the same. In the interview, I (PE) ask the questions and my mother (VB) answers them.

PE: 'I was going to ask you about the First World War, because you were fourteen years old then.'

VB: 'I remember about all these young lads, going to join up. I remember Kitchener's poster, He was pointing a finger out: 'Your country needs you'. Minchinhampton Band were marching round the streets and these young lads behind, only eighteen or nineteen, because they wouldn't have them under eighteen, with their mothers there … a lot of them never came back.'

PE: 'When they went off, they were volunteers?'

VB: 'Yes, in those days.'

PE: 'And the officers were the local gentry.'

VB: 'Yes. And you could buy a commission in those days; anyone that had money could buy a commission.'

PE: 'So they went off, these lads, and what happened when they died?'

VB: 'A lot of them were killed, and a lot of them were taken prisoner. The parents were informed that their son had been killed, one after the other, people got the letters to notify that their sons had been killed.'

PE: 'And they were all in the Gloucestershire Regiment?'

VB: 'The 8th Gloucesters, most of them.'

PE: 'So they all belonged to the same group.'

VB: 'Most of them did.'

PE: 'So, if there was a group of people involved in a particular battle, and it was a bloody battle, then they were all killed?'

VB: 'Oh, there were a lot from Minchinhampton killed.'

PE: 'Do you remember the reaction in the village at that time?'

VB: 'Yes, it was dreadful, really.'

PE: 'What sort of reaction? What used to happen?'

VB: 'I don't know that anything happened. They were quiet about it, they never made a fuss but they just mourned about them.'

PE: 'Were there services in the church?'

VB: 'Yes, we used to have services in the church, every week there was a service.'

PE: 'For boys who were killed?'

VB: 'Yes, and about the war.'

PE: 'They used to mention the names of those who were killed?'

VB: 'Yes, they used to call out the names, one after the other, nice young lads they were.'

PE: 'And you knew them?'

VB: 'Oh yes I did. I knew them all.'

PE: 'What did you think?'

VB: 'Well, it was very depressing, really. Especially when they used to come home on leave and then they'd have to go back.'

PE: 'Because you knew that if they went back they might not come home again?'

VB: 'Oh yes, you did. They were all in the trenches, they had a terrible time.'

PE: 'Did they talk about it?'

VB: 'Not a lot really.'

PE: 'Were they quiet boys?'

VB: 'Yes. They never made a fuss about it.'

PE: 'What did they think, that they were doing their duty?'

VB: 'They thought so, yes.'

PE: 'And what did they think they were fighting for?'

VB: 'I don't know what they thought. But I knew that they volunteered to go, and I know that one or two who weren't passed to do so were really upset because they couldn't go to be with their friends.'

PE: 'And all these friends went together?'

VB: 'Yes.'

PE: 'And after the war, the survivors came back, and there was a lot of unemployment, wasn't there?'

VB: 'Yes, there was a lot of unemployment. Of course your father was out in Germany with the army of occupation.'

It is difficult for us now to imagine the horror those young men went through. Two spared from the slaughter came back with a bayonet to present to my grandfather, with the blood of a German on it. My grandmother gave food to a mother and her children whose father, a sergeant, had been killed. The children scavenged in the streets for something to eat.

Poems tell us much, particularly one which has become famous, 'In Flanders Fields'. It was written by a Canadian doctor, Lieutenant Colonel John McCrae, on 3 May 1915, after conducting the funeral of his friend and fellow soldier Alexis Helmer, who died in the Second Battle of Ypres. 'In Flanders Fields' was first published on 8 December of that year in the magazine *Punch*. Its references to the red poppies that grew over the graves of fallen soldiers resulted in those flowers becoming the world's most recognized memorial symbols of the war dead.

For me, born between the First and Second World Wars, the shadow of the first grew into the second. My mother would take me to tea with friends who would never marry as so many men had been killed. A single woman who worked for the *Church Times*, Rosamund Essex, later told me how she had adopted a son, because she knew she would never marry. I remember being much taken by the memorial in Brimscombe cemetery to the Cole brothers and thinking as a child what a loss it must have been.

I gradually became aware of the war – partly through emblems drawn in my mother's autograph book by Australians at Aston Down in 1918 of their native territories. What I did not know then was how that connection would grow in my life, lasting even now with a real life story, centred on Brimscombe, of romance over two generations, daring and tragedy.

On the wall of a neighbour's living room in Victoria Road was a picture that caught my imagination as a child. She said it was of her Australian relatives, a nephew and niece. They were dressed up as Romans for a carnival. I did not know that, and thought for a long time it was the Australian national costume. Years later, she told me that the boy, Bob Clark, now a young man, was coming to stay with her. He told me the family story. His father was a pilot at Aston Down, who led fighter planes low over Piccadilly to celebrate the end of the First World War. He married a local girl and took her to Australia. He went to work in New Guinea with the Australian administration, bringing with him his family, who were evacuated back to Australia before the Japanese came. They never saw him again.

Grampy Evans took me as a 7 year old to look at Aston Down after it was opened as an RAF base in 1938. I cycled there during the war and saw the aircraft coming and going, my interest in flying and aerial warfare awakened by the Aussies in the First World War and by the Battle of Britain.

Later I saw a Swastika paraded in Brimscombe, covering the coffin of a German airman, Georg W. Theiner, brought down near Oakridge. He was buried with full military honours by the RAF in our hillside cemetery, with a salute fired at his graveside. The memory stayed with me. During my National Service in the Cold War on an operational Bomber Command station, RAF Wyton, I lost two aircrew friends. One was a pilot, Flight Lieutenant Ken Watson, who won the Distinguished Flying Cross in the war for bravery. He could have bailed out from his blazing Canberra but he stayed put because his navigator was trapped and couldn't escape. Ken's last words heard over the radio to his navigator, John Wilson, were a calm: 'Goodbye John, this is it.'

My other friend, Gordon Naldrett, was navigator in a specially equipped Canberra on its way over the Pacific to fly through the fumes of an H-Bomb test. The top-secret mission was arranged by Churchill with the Americans and planned in the office next to mine. Naldrett's Canberra disappeared en route.

I was thus fired up when the Mayor of Dresden objected to the provision of a Bomber Command memorial to its 55,000 volunteer aircrew who died on operations. Retired after thirty years on *The Times* and a subscriber now, I cited in the paper the wartime funeral with honours of Georg W. Theiner in Brimscombe, although he had come to bomb and kill.

The First World War was supposedly the war to end all wars. But that was not true for Brimscombe any more than for anywhere else. Lieutenant Arthur Peal, who lived up Brimscombe Hill, was one of the Glorious Glosters in the heroic Imjin river stand in the Korean War. He was taken prisoner and every week I visited his mother with Red Cross pictures of captive soldiers received in the *Stroud News* to see if we could identify him. Brimscombe celebrated when he eventually came home.

As a small boy my father, Stanley, watched a procession up Brimscombe Hill in 1900, led by a band, to celebrate the relief of Mafeking in the Boer War. I now find myself giving talks and writing about international terrorism, which I have been covering for the last fifty years. Action I took as a *Times* journalist caught a terrorist from the then most murderous gang in Europe, which was involved in the hijacking of an airliner. But that's another story about yet another war.

Until the Second World War, childhood in Brimscombe was much the same as my father experienced before the First. Music was taught to us both. Like the great organist Albert Schweitzer, he played for his first church service at the age

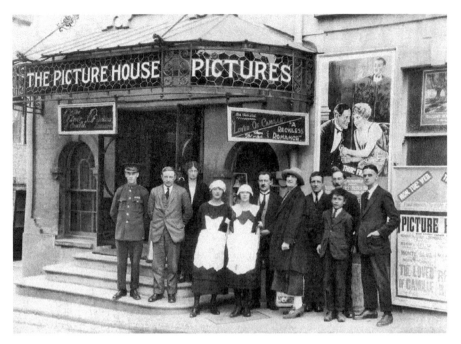

The Picture House in Stroud. The film being advertised dates this photograph to 1924. (Author's collection)

of 9. Tribute to him was paid later by his teacher, Samuel Underwood, organist at Stroud parish church and conductor of the Stroud, Bristol and Swindon choral societies, as well as the Gloucester Orpheus Choir. He said my father was the only organist he had come across who could sight-read a Bach fugue, using the pedals as well.

This came in useful after the war when he was organist at the Stroud Picture House in the great days of silent films. He received the music on a Monday morning with the film and had to match it with movement and drama on the screen in the afternoon. There were other instrumentalists, including a couple trained in the Brussels Conservatoire.

My father never realised his full potential. He was organist in turn at churches in Brimscombe, Chalford and Holy Trinity, Stroud. The Bishop of Tewkesbury once offered him a grammar school teaching post and opportunity in local music, but he stayed in Brimscombe all his life, unlike his cousin, Elsie Chambers. Trained by Ivor Novello's mother and Sir Henry Wood, founder of the Proms, she achieved national recognition as a contralto and sang to the troops in France in the First World War.

She said that when she took part in a concert for the 51st Highland Division she realised many of the men sitting before her would never see home again.

She sang homely songs. She was good at matching music to her audience, as she did when singing to people in the East End of London and in Liverpool.

My father, who was in the Royal Engineers, later as a despatch rider on a motorbike, also joined a concert party. On his bike in Cologne after the war, he met Elsie by chance in the street. He bore a scar to the end of his life on his upper lip from injury in a crash when he swerved off the road to avoid a small German boy running into it, to the enormous thanks of his mother. His experience with Germans while in the army led him to hire two German prisoners from a camp at Aston Down at the end of the Second World War, to work in the garden of Lewiston House, then our home. They were paid with cigarettes and, although we were still rationed, shared a meal. One, a baker, was more amenable than the other and said he had not wished to join the army. When he returned home, he sent us a religious book as a Christmas present, with his good wishes.

After the First World War, recitals my father gave with Elsie in Brimscombe church attracted so many that an overflow audience outside listened to the music, reaching them through opened doors.

The churches then were a focus for much activity in the community. My father moved from Brimscombe to Chalford when the vicar, the Revd E.D. Panter, rebuked him for going after the service for a drink in the Yew Tree, then on the Pike – 'the thirst after righteousness', as it was known. He did not see anything wrong with it and hated, too, interference with his choice of music for organ voluntaries, which was not always narrowly religious.

As a child I never knew what would happen next in our household. I was born in my grandparents' house, where they had lived since the nineteenth century. They were joined by my parents after their marriage. Uncle Albert, Grannie Evans's brother, who lived in London defying the blitz, has his name in gold in the tower at Chalford church for ringing innumerable changes in peals on the steel bells.

Poster for an Elsie Chambers concert at Stroud Subscription Rooms in 1921. (Author's collection)

He played several brass instruments, including a trumpet. Ramrod erect, he wore medal ribbons from the Boer and the First World War.

Another great uncle, Arty, was a ventriloquist, entertaining children in his spare time. He took me by surprise when a figure, not much smaller than I was at the time, popped up from a box and began talking to me. Elsie would come and sing German Lieder to my father's accompaniment. He would play a Beethoven sonata. Both Grannie and Grampy Evans played the violin but were not virtuosos. Zoura, Elsie's sister, had a watercolour hung in the Royal Academy's summer exhibition. Zoura's first job was with the Red Bus Company, started by an Aston Down Australian who stayed here after the war. She later moved to work at Erinoid, where she set up and ran their technical library.

Ever a performer, one day Grannie dressed up as a tramp and went along the road with primitive so-called 'theatrical' make-up on her face and asked Mr Williams three doors away in broadest Gloucestershire: 'Can you tell I the way to Stroud?' Completely taken in, he told her.

Ours was a Victorian household. I was born dead there. I have a tape recording of my mother repeating the words of Dr Alfred Brown who blew breath into me for twenty minutes before I began to breathe: 'Mrs Evans, I will not only congratulate you on having a son, but a son who is alive.' When he died I was asked to write his obituary in the *Stroud News*, where he had intervened with the editor, one of his patients, to get me my first job. I called on his widow to get background facts and told her what he had done for me. Tears came to her eyes. Dr Brown's Road in Minchinhampton was named after him by grateful patients.

The Victorian influence meant that my grandfather forbade me 'blood and thunder' comics like *Hotspur*, *Wizard* and *Champion* although I did a black market deal with a boy up the road to get them second hand. Instead I was given a wholesome *Chatterbox* annual from the turn of the nineteenth century. For my birthday I had *The Pilgrim's Progress*. Sunday school in the afternoon was between matins and evensong in my father's church choir.

To protect me after my hesitant start in life folk remedies were applied from a handwritten book handed down from a great-grandfather, which included a recipe for welding cast steel. Grannie Evans woke me at 7 a.m. with a raw onion to eat to ward away germs. My father produced chest expanders – tubular-shaped stiff springs, pulled apart with effort by handles at each end – for repeated exercises. I have broad shoulders as a result. In the 1960s when tattooing was looking like dying out, I went as a *Times* correspondent to interview the last practitioner in Plymouth. 'Stop!' he said, as I entered the door. 'I have been waiting for someone like you. You have a broad enough back. I'll do the Last

Supper on it for £8!' That was a bargain even in those days, but I didn't fancy lying on the beach as a religious art exhibition.

In Brimscombe in my father's day, use of dialect was still strong, and it lingered in my childhood with hints of a Saxon origin. In 'bist thee one of they?' ('are you one of them?') the word 'bist' tallies with the German I learned a school. Evidence shows that the family has lived in Minchinhampton, father to son, for at least 600 years and is still there.

My mother recalled that in the days before radio and instant information, news of the sinking of the *Titanic* in 1912 was brought to Minchinhampton by a villager running through the streets and shouting, 'S'welp me god, the Tintack's gone down.'

Ernie Barrett was the much respected last captain of the volunteer Brimscombe village fire brigade – I don't think they could afford a horse. He was also vicar's warden at the church. Its annual fête in the vicarage garden was greatly enjoyed by children led up Brimscombe Hill in procession by a uniformed band. Mr Barrett always proposed a vote of thanks: 'It be very kind of the dear vicar, to have us yer, yer by yer.'

Courtesy demanded that the invitation be extended to Cotswold characters known for miles around, like George and Dorcas Juggins. They had a donkey and cart, but how they survived financially was always a bit of a mystery. One day the donkey dropped down dead. 'He hasn't done that before,' said George.

Some businesses are vital, like undertaking, and fulfil obvious demand, but there's fierce competition. Ernie Brown's business was in death, but he lived life to the full. In his 60s, after his wife died, he wooed and married Elizabeth, a young village lady, and a new family was started.

Ernie, up with the times, insisted he be called a funeral director. One day he announced a competitive edge over local rivals, a chapel of ease, where the dead could rest in peace. 'It's a second-hand Batley (prefabricated) garage,' he said, 'down by the canal.' He had installed an altar – a table covered in a green baize cloth, dignified with two candlesticks on it, donated by the vicar of the neighbouring village, Chalford.

'Come and have a look,' he said, opening the door. The floor of concrete screed was still unfinished. On it were two open coffins, one with a pair of children sitting in it, his, the other occupied by two friends. 'We're Oxford, they're Cambridge,' one said, emulating the annual inter-university boat race, as with makeshift oars they rowed towards the altar.

With the quiet, insistent dignity that undertakers have, Ernie ushered me gently towards the door, changing the subject discreetly. He sniffed the air, which had a marked chill in it. 'I'll have to be ordering some more coffin wood,' he said, a master of business opportunity.

I was a small child when I first met Ernie. He was lying on the ground with a broken leg at the side of the road in Brimscombe Hill, knocked down by a cyclist. A village teaches you how to get on with all sorts of people in all sorts of circumstances. He died before his second wife, whom I later met sitting by herself at a village school reunion. 'You liked Ernie?' she asked a little hesitantly when I sat beside her. 'Yes,' I said. 'Very much. He was a very human being and I was glad to know him.'

As a 9 year old I had as much freedom as my father did, much more than more fearful parents allow today. The hills were there to roam. My gang's territory was the moors, just a path up a small hill if you didn't know them. But bows and arrows could be cut from the hedgerows below, which provided branches to make a shelter. A narrow stream, gushing beneath lavish trees for us to climb, allowed me to sail the *Admiral Graf Spee*, in real life defeated in the Battle of the River Plate, bumping against the sides of the stream which took it along, until it heeled over – as the real *Admiral Graf Spee* was scuttled in defeat.

All was well in our make-believe world until with a fearsome shout Farmer Halliday came after us brandishing a stick. We scattered double quick. We left behind as a decoy an even smaller boy, obviously harmless, and hid behind a wall watching. Visibly nonplussed, Mr Halliday took the small boy by the hand up the hill and down the road to his home. Next day Farmer Halliday appeared as usual with a yoke over his shoulders bearing a pail of milk on each side. I stood next to my mother when she opened the door. 'Good morning, Mrs Evans.' 'Good morning, Mr Halliday. Two pints, please.' There was never a hint from Mr Halliday or me of the previous evening's conflict.

The small boy grew up to be a soldier. He was pictured in recruiting posters up and down the land and in newspaper advertisements, obviously having been well trained early on.

The village had a shortage of flat land, except for one field next to our road with a gentle slope down to it for sliding on trays in snow. A boy who kept goal there, between two piles of jumpers as 'posts', later played for Bristol Rovers.

Running down to the hedge at the bottom of the field overlooking the railway, I could see the white smoke streaming from the funnel of the record-breaking *Cheltenham Flyer* as it thundered up the valley past me, making me proud to be British.

That was in the late 1930s, when Hitler marched into neighbouring land to gain *Lebensraum*. To my 7-year-old mind trying to understand the six o'clock news, the local council was after *Lebensraum* too. Its surveyors pegged out our field to show where houses should be built. One dark night I stole down and pulled out the pegs. I overheard that it was put down to hooligans. The field remained free for play until the threat of bombing. As patriots we had no objection when trenches were dug there to provide shelter against a blitz that never came. Nor when, as part of the war effort, Britain was urged to 'Dig for Victory' and the field was covered in allotments. I had saved it for the nation. Not until long after the war were houses built there.

The wars took the lives of village men and disturbed the lives of others. Nightly a demobbed soldier, his mind battle torn, shouted orders at a phantom squad at 2 a.m. Nobody complained. The boy next door lost his father. Jim Prime, another young village man who sang in the church choir, died while in the hands of the Japanese.

The wars demanded much understanding, tolerance and stoicism. Brimscombe, to its credit, provided them.

ACKNOWLEDGEMENTS AND SELECTED SOURCES

Chief sources of information were local papers – the *Stroud News* and the *Stroud Journal*, which at the time of the Great War were separate publications (the *News* the more right-wing of the two). The papers (randomly *News* or *Journal*) are available on microfiche in Stroud Library, but while we were in the thick of our researches, some old bound volumes of the actual newspapers emerged from the offices of the *Stroud News and Journal*, which was being redecorated. Three of these were *Journals*, for years for which we had only had *News*es, and provided much supplementary information (and excitement!). We are grateful to the *Stroud News and Journal* for its help and permission to use photographs and to quote from it. Other papers consulted included the *Gloucestershire Echo*, the *Citizen*, the *Cheltenham Chronicle* and the *Gloucester Gazette*.

We are also grateful for the warm and studious surroundings of Gloucestershire Archives, where we were able to read original documents such as school log-books, parish magazines, minutes of meetings and scrapbooks of cuttings.

The Soldiers of Gloucestershire Museum in Gloucester has provided information and insights.

Much of our biographical information was gleaned from Internet sites, including the Commonwealth War Graves (www.cwgc.org), Ancestry (www. ancestry.co.uk), and Find My Past (www.findmypast.co.uk).

Some of the local history societies are blessed with access to unpublished memoirs and reminiscences.

The photograph collections of Howard Beard and Mike Mills, generously shared, have inspired and enthralled us.

Useful books include:

Atkinson, Gillian, *A Photographic History of Standish House and its Occupants*, 2004

Blackman, Tina, *The Three Uncles: The Cole Brothers in the Great War*, The Choir Press, 2014

Fetherston-Godley, Lady Kathleen, *Lest We Forget: World War 1, 1914–1918 Book of Remembrance*, presented to Royal British Legion Stonehouse Branch 1921. (Original is in Gloucestershire Archives, and a copy with Stonehouse History Group)

Kelly's Directory 1914

Loosley, S.G.H., *Wycliffe College: The First Hundred Years, 1882–1982*, Gomer Press, 1982

Sibly, W.A. & Newth, J.D. (eds), *Wycliffe and the War*, privately printed by John Bellows, 1923

The Stroud District and its Part in the Great War 1914–1919, the Stroud News Publishing Co. Ltd, 1919 (also reprinted with a modern introduction by Charles Townley, Stroud History Publications, 2010)

Specific sources for Minchinhampton Aerodrome:

Australian War Memorial (www.awm.gov.au)

David Goodland and Alan Vaughan, *Anzacs over England*, Alan Sutton, 1992

James M. Woolley, *Aussies over the Cotswolds*, James Woolley, 1992

Original collection of the late Malcolm Gay

The destination for history
www.thehistorypress.co.uk